"The heart is the seat of intuitive knowledge and receiver of Divine instruction. It is truly magnificent."

THE MAGNIFICENT ORGAN

The Heart of Quran, Hadith,
Science, and Wholistic
Healing Experiences

JEANETTE HABLULLAH, N.D.

Olive Media Services ~ Columbia, MO

THE MAGNIFICENT ORGAN

The Heart of Quran, Hadith, Science, and Wholistic Healing Experiences

Printed in the United States of America

ISBN 0-9707831-2-4

PUBLISHED BY:

Olive Media Services
PO Box 30762
Columbia, MO 65205-3762
www.omspublishing.com

DEDICATION

For the five hearts that began a sweet rhythm in a sacred place and still beat strongly by permission of our Loving, Compassionate Lord.

For my children, Elisa Anne, Rochelle Lee, Ronnie Leonard, Ayanna Nalini, and Joshua.

May the supreme desire of your hearts be granted.

Amin.

EXPRESSIONS OF GRATITUDE

Subhana Allahu wa bi hamdihi. Subhana Allah Al-Azeem. Glory to The One God and all Praise is for Him. Glory to The One God, The Magnificent. Praise is for Allah and all thankfulness. And this spirit of thankfulness, appreciation, and gratitude must be extended to Allah's creation. It is with that spirit that I acknowledge and convey extreme gratitude to those who have assisted me to bring what began as an understanding to completion in the form of a book.

First I will mention the students of Electrical Engineering at Sudan University of Science and Technology, for it was while teaching them English in 1998 that this light of understanding began to manifest. Second are my friends and family with whom I have shared conversations and received ideas which helped develop themes, particularly Sr. Nuurah Muhammed with whom I shared a daily email conversation during most of this writing.

My book would not have been as well written as it is if it had not been for the editorial and religious commentary and suggestions from my close friend Sr. Khadija Haffajee, Br. Shakir Al-Ani, and my daughter Ayanna. Working from primitive research methods I spent long hours searching for Quranic Ayat and Hadith. My son-in law, Tariq Shalabi, was extremely helpful in this area. He called upon his personal knowledge and sought additional help when needed from Dr. Ali Bagegni, and others.

There was much encouragement to complete this work and what you hold in your hands as you read is the work of many. The adaptation to book form and the printing process was supervised by Ayanna. May Allah reward her, for I surely am not prepared for such tasks and avoid spending my time and brain space on them. Before ending I must give a special appreciation to the cover artist, a young university student, who took her time making drafts and revisions, and asked nothing in return.

The Arabic text was another challenge. Yet, I was determined that this work not be published without it. May Allah generously reward all of those who were on stand by willing to help if needed.

Allah is the best of Knowers and the best to reward. Jazakum Allahu khairan katheeran (May Allah reward you all generously) for every effort, thought and moment you spent in helping *The Magnificent Organ* get to this stage.

Was salaamu alaikum wa rahmatullahi wa barakatuhu,

Jeanette Habibullah

FOREWORD

In our everyday lexicon the word "heart" is used to flaunt, taunt, and play on our emotions. How often have we heard the following expressions: "have a heart", "a heavy heart", "wear your heart on your sleeve", "hard-hearted", "from the bottom of my heart", "have one's heart in the right place", "near to one's heart". All of these have been used at some point by someone to express feelings. Now there is a book "The Magnificent Organ: The Heart of Quran, Hadith and Wholistic Healing Experiences". Herein is a new way of looking at and understanding the heart, not only as a vital organ, a physical entity, but also as the source of judgment and wisdom providing a balance between thought and action.

When I was asked to edit this book some months ago, I was intrigued by both the title and the approach used by the author. I did so with pleasure, as I have known Sr. Jeanette and worked with her on projects for almost two decades. We have also engaged in long discussions on matters spiritual. Later she asked me to write this foreword. I consider this a privilege, especially as it is a book written by a Muslim female.

Islam is a comprehensive system that addresses all aspects of our life. Unfortunately, being weak, we have tended to reduce this most special way of life to the lowest common denominator of a set of legalistic rituals. This Deen, that our Lord and Creator has entrusted to us, is greater than we are and our limited knowledge and understanding of it is indicative of the dilemma we as Muslims are facing today.

In the Qur'an, Allah (SWT) draws our attention to all aspects of our life, as physical beings with an intellect as well as emotions and most importantly as spiritual persons. We are reminded, "It is He Who brought you forth from the wombs of your mothers, when you knew nothing, and He gave you hearing and sight and intelligence and affections that you may give thanks" (Quran 16:78). It is logical, therefore, that when we reject His way "Allah hath set a seal on their heart and on their hearing and on their eyes is a veil" (Quran 2:7).

Sr. Jeanette has used the Quranic approach to present to us how her experience as a Wholistic Healer helped her to a deeper insight into the working of the heart. She explains how Allah (SWT) has created us as physical, mental and spiritual beings. Our responsibility is to understand ourselves first, because it is only when we do this, that we can help our community. In a world where technology is king and humans have not kept up the pace, we do not have the time to address our needs as spiritual beings.

This book has seven chapters in all. It is an interesting read. Chapters One and Two set the stage by giving us the fundamental theoretical information about the link between the heart and brain.

There are references from the Quran as well as researched sources from the sciences to help us understand what happens when we fail to balance between the aggressive brain and the calm, gentle heart and ignore or reject the Truth. Emphasis is on the working of the heart.

In Chapter Three the author presents new material about factors that may lead to heart diseases. The physical illness is affected by what she calls "a disconnected Spirit". If there is the absence of Islam, Iman or Taqwa, then the "security and safety" of the individual are missing. The rebellion against Allah is a state of neglect of the spirit which leads to a corrupted heart. The process is discussed in Chapter Four, together with ways to a healthy heart.

The next Chapter, "Rhythms Of The Heart" tells about the effects of sounds in Nature and all around us. There are the pure sounds, which are a joy to hear and bring calmness and others that are impure and noisy. She then establishes the link between sound and healing.

Chapter Six is a very practical discussion on our daily interactions with others in many places: home, work and other social settings and how these impact on our spiritual wellness. The final Chapter appropriately ensures us that "Peacefulness of the heart is the greatest treasure we can acquire".

This book is a long awaited addition to the bookshelves of both Muslim and non-Muslims with some very thought provoking ideas on how we see ourselves — beyond our physical bodies. Yet, it includes detailed explanations on the physiology of the brain-heart connection and how it affects our health, both physical and spiritual.

May Allah (SWT) reward the efforts of Sr. Jeanette and insha Allah those who read this book and remember to say the supplication of Prophet Muhammad (pbuh), "Oh Allah, change our hearts, change our hearts to be obedient to You" and "Oh Allah, I seek refuge in You from perversity and anxiety and I seek refuge in You from aspiring after that which is beyond aspiration."

Khadija Haffajee
Ottawa, Ontario, Canada
October 2000 / Rajab 1421

TABLE OF CONTENTS

INTRODUCTION

With the name of Allah, the Merciful, the Compassionate

أَفَلَمْ يَسِيرُوا فِى ٱلْأَرْضِ
فَتَكُونَ لَهُمْ قُلُوبٌ يَعْقِلُونَ بِهَآ أَوْ ءَاذَانٌ يَسْمَعُونَ بِهَآ فَإِنَّهَا
لَا تَعْمَى ٱلْأَبْصَٰرُ وَلَٰكِن تَعْمَى ٱلْقُلُوبُ ٱلَّتِى فِى ٱلصُّدُورِ ۝

*"Do they not travel through the land so that their
hearts (and minds) may thus learn wisdom, and
their ears may thus learn to hear? Truly it is not
their eyes that are blind, but their hearts which are
in their chests." (Quran 22:46)*

Alhamdulillahi al 'Aleem, al Hakeem. Praise be to Allah the All

Knowing, the Wise. We seek assistance from Him, we ask

forgiveness of Him and we beseech His guidance. As many

scientists, students and people of knowledge have come to realize,

scientific facts have given confirmation to and support for the

divine information given generously by Allah (swt) in the Quran.

15

Maurice Bucaille, a French scientist, documented many of these inseparable partnerships in his popular book "The Bible, The Quran, and Science" and others have similarly written and lectured. Of such topics, there are none more fascinating and beautiful than those concerning the heart. On the frequent occasions when your attention must have been drawn to the heart, you have certainly recalled some of what is stored in your personal information system. You might have immediately thought of it as a physical organ, residing in the chest cavity and perhaps even visualized its appearance with the tubelike arteries and veins connected, filled with surging, liquid life. If the thought stimulus was more of an emotional nature it may have evoked remembrances of love, joy or pain which would then have taken your thoughts on any variety of paths. Usually our heart centered sessions are brief, unless unfortunate circumstances force us to deliver prolonged attention due to heart disease, circulatory problems or the wounded heart of disappointment, rejection, separation or abandonment.

Yet, the heart is and has always been central to our physical and spiritual existence. Giving consideration to knowledge from both revelation and science will, at once, stimulate intellectual curiosity and spur a reflective investigation. Indulging both desires can result in a calm quenching of the thirst of the mind and spirit. The heart is a sign of the magnificence of our creation. It links the spiritual and the physical, the apparent and the obscure, the perceptible and the imperceptible. It defies a truly adequate explanation and yet volumes have been written on its significance and function. These writings are not limited to any specific field as you will find chapters in scientific/medical texts, numerous metaphysical and psychological references and beautiful poems and spiritual meditations written to extol the power and depth of the heart.

During 1998, I read fascinating articles relating new scientific research and discoveries concerning the heart and also listened to tapes about the expanded power and realm of the heart. These caused me to reflect back on the Ayahs (Quranic verses) in which Allah uses the term qalb (heart) and also on hadith (sayings of the Prophet Muhammad). The connection between

17

revealed words, inspired words, and new scientific insights is awe inspiring and spiritually satisfying. Thus on October 16, 1998 I began this small book in a humble attempt to bring Quran, Hadith and current scientific, documented information together and share what has come to be clear to me about the heart. Where applicable I will also share my personal experiences from the practice of wholistic healing which only serve to exemplify the truth of the other information.

May Allah (swt) have mercy upon me and provide me with words of clarity and enable me to transfer to you, the reader, some of the magnificence of this subject. Amin.

Jeanette Hablullah

May 2000 / Safar 1421

Preface

Throughout the text certain Arabic terms and abbreviations are used because their use is universally common.

Allah is used instead of the English God

swt = subhanahu wa ta'alaa (glorified and exalted is He); used after the name of Allah.

iwj = 'Izza wa Jala (The Great and Magnificent); used after the name of Allah.

saw = salla Allahu alaihi wa salam (may Allah exalt him and give him peace); used after the name of Prophet Muhammad

Translated verses of Quran are based on an updated English translation and commentary of the Quran by Abdullah Yusuf Ali. When warranted minor changes in wording were made in order to facilitate readability while retaining the correctness of the Arabic Text.

"A true "heart to heart" conversation will yield all the truth we need."

Chapter One

Biology and Beyond

"I have little doubt that the heart is the major energy center of my body and a conveyor of a code that represents my soul."

Dr. Paul Pearsall

The cardiovascular system is one of the first systems to form in the developing embryo. Its remarkable development is first apparent at the nineteenth day as a mass of specialized cells. A mere six days later, it has developed a rhythm and pumping action by which it delivers nutrients and disposes of wastes via the interaction with maternal blood vessels in the placenta. Its primary component, the heart, is the cardiovascular version of an inextricable aspect of creation; the existence of mutually complementing opposites (i.e. day and night, male and female, etc.) With its systolic – diastolic, contracting – relaxing action and its side by side pumps, it performs and directs a continuous, harmonious coordination of opposite yet complementary universal energy (yin-yang). The left pump, amazingly powerful, services thousands of miles of vessels while the right is mainly concerned with the oxygenation process. By nature the heart is integrative. It develops by a process of fusion[1] as the cells merge together during development. This process establishes junctions between the cells and multiple nuclei and allows intercellular electrical communication that brings all of the heart cells into one accord. Once this process is complete, the heat unites all other cells of the developing fetus in their dependence upon it for life support. While it is an integrative and interactive organ it remains semi-independent in the origin of its rhythmic and muscular function. Quoting an anatomy text, "Cardiac muscle possesses an intrinsic rhythmicity that allows the heart-beat to originate in and be conducted through the heart without extrinsic stimulation." [2] No one can be sure about the source of the heart's rhythm, though it has been suggested for some years now that the developing heart must get it impulse and rhythm from the mother's own heartbeat. However, that means, with retroactive determination of origin, that our hearts rhythm was set by the rhythm of the hearts of Adam and Hawwa (Eve) who were tuned to the rhythm that the Creator (swt) had established for the human creation. In other words our hearts are tuned to the Creator's own chosen rhythm.

Heart cells combine to form a tireless and powerful muscle, unlike any other muscle in the human body. Individually and collectively the cells do what no other cells in the human body do-they pulsate. The pulsation is the result of a subtle and, as yet, immeasurable (unable to be charted by machines in the manner of electroencephalograms-EEG's or electrocardiograms-ECG's) energy which is now being labeled as L-energy or life energy meaning it is the most basic energy of all living matter. This is the energy which sets the billions of heart cells in motion and infuses them with an Electro-Magnetic Field (EMF) which has been measured as 5000 times stronger than the EMF created by the brain.[3] Its biophysical energy, measured in electrocardiograms, travels throughout the entire body and can be electronically recorded at any point on the body and even several feet away.

This fact has interesting implications in considering the effect of one's heart energy on other individuals or energy systems outside of the body's own boundaries. It has already been shown that the ECG pattern of one heart can be measured in the electroencephalogram (EEG) of the brain of another individual nearby.[4] Every cell in the body is permeated with this energy coming from and generated by the heart. Electromagnetic energy travels at the speed of light. This indicates that the function of every one of the trillions of cells in the human body is simultaneously influenced with every beat of the heart and that the quality of that energy will directly affect the physiological condition and function.

The Heart's Electrical Nature

The heart's ability to and responsibility for supplying the entire system with energy makes it the body's main power generator. Science has long known of the electrical nature of the body and that there are positive and negative poles through which energy is conducted. The system of acupuncture in Oriental

Medicine is based on meridians or currents of energy that run through the body. Anatomical designs of the entire neurological system render it similar to complex electrical wiring through which messages are conducted by charged particles (ions). In the physical body the heart represents the negative pole and the brain the positive. This sets a perfect conduit/pathway for the remarkable flow of energy between them, which proceeds naturally from the negative (pole) to the positive (pole). This pattern, along with the fact that the heart's power is so much greater than that of the brain, is enough to show that the heart will naturally exert more influence on the brain than the brain will on the heart.

Beyond the long established neurological connections between these two entities (via the autonomic nervous system), there is now another established link. Neurotransmitters, cells once thought to be exclusive to the brain, have been identified in the heart, thus establishing a basis for neurochemical and electrochemical communication. In fact, researchers at the National Institute of Mental Health report that there is evidence that the heart requests an update from the brain in order to properly direct the body's energy level.[5] These two must harmonize their functions for the healthy, whole existence of the human being. The union of body, mind and spirit, which is man in his harmonious totality, is only achieved in this way. The brain is uniquely prepared to receive electrical impulses from the physical environment by way of the sensory organs and to code, categorize, integrate, and store that information. It also has a certain ability to "think" or analyze data, giving support to the theory that the brain's primary evolutionary purpose is to direct the physical system for survival and self-improvement. The heart on the other hand has a more expansive realm. It links the physical with the spiritual – emotional and is truly the master conductor of the body until and unless its direction is overruled.

The electrical relationship between the brain and the heart has been mechanically recorded by studies at the Institute of Heart Math (IHM) in Boulder Creek, California. There, they have electrically recorded patterns in heart energy being affected by mental thoughts. Heart patterns that recorded as negative or damaging were calmed into healthy patterns by invoking memories of happiness, serenity, appreciation etc. This verified change in dominant energy clearly demonstrates the interdependent nature of these two organs, as the heart reflects what you allow to dominate in your conscious mind. Here I am going to venture beyond that concept and suggest that the heart prompts the change when the dominating energy has gone into a negative state. I say that because every state of fear, anger, frustration, etc. has a period in which it is normal and perhaps even beneficial. However, extended periods of these emotions, generally tagged as negative, or unnecessary surges of the same due to stress become destructive to the heart and the entire biological system as harmful hormones surge through the bloodstream. The heart in its position of governance and maintenance of a healthy system is responsible to call for a change and will do just that. What the researchers at the IHM have shown is that all you have to do is re-center your attention from the head/brain to the heart area and recall a pleasant experience in order to "freeze" the negative and allow the positive to enter .[6] At that point, they say you can ask for a suggestion as to how to better handle the situation and it will come to you. This act of consulting the heart for wisdom and guidance is ancient and more detail will be given to this topic in Chapter 2.

Heart To Brain

The heart and brain are meant to function in harmonious coordination. Yet an old and common advice was "Think with your head and not with your heart" and "Use your head." Isn't it ironic that some contemporary proponents of health and wisdom are now advising just the opposite. The truth is that, although the heart does have a brain of its own that is an organized network of nerve cells and nerve plexi[7], it relies on information collected by the brain via the sensory organs. When all of these organs are working, the eyes are the primary information receptors. Light waves of varying lengths and vibrations enter through the eye into an extremely complex system of nerves. When the heart is more open, the eyes respond. The pupils dilate allowing more energy information to enter and record in the occipital region from where it is retrieved by the heart. The brain then is acting as a "servant" of the heart, which is how it is viewed in Oriental Medicine. In that system the brain is labeled as a "curious organ" and the heart as "the Emperor" or the center and ruler of all activity. [8]

While you may not choose to respect or accept the oriental philosophy, the truth is that one can be "brain dead" and still live. Life is essentially the ability of the heart to maintain its rhythm. When this is lost, life cannot continue. But, life in its fullness and completeness is living with the guidance of a heart and brain in resonant submission to the Glorious and Glorified Creator. So, for those seekers of increased and enhanced brain power, it is not to be achieved by focusing solely on the brain and consuming brain enhancing herbs, elixirs, etc. Results achieved in this way are illusory and incomplete. The brain is at its greatest capacity when it works in synchronized activity with the heart. This is how researchers at IHM say "cortical facilitation" is effected[9] or how more power and intelligence are made available to the brain.

When the brain functions alone, its character is definitely aggressive. This is evidenced in the rapid evolution of industry and technology. It demands attention, stimulation and material manifestations of its abilities. Left without restraints or guidance it can also engage the self in a constant dialogue, which often is nonsense chatter precluding peace of mind and even sleep. Numerous individuals seeking to silence the demands and chaotic ramblings of the brain resort to medication, while others retreat to meditative prayer and remembrances of the spirit. As Allah ta'alaa says in Quran,

"Man will have what he strives for." [10]

Our brains have created numerous extensions of them-selves, the most definitive example being the computer. We have advanced technology at breakneck speed; to the point that human (resource) development cannot keep pace. We have stressed ourselves to the point that, as of March 1999, the statistical reports indicate there are 1,000 heart attacks every hour somewhere in the United States.[11] For this, our wonderful brains have created portable fibrillators, little boxes with extension tubes which can deliver an electric jolt to the heart to get it beating again.

The brain is functional and efficient. It is not cruel, just void of the ability to make compassionate judgment that considers the benefit of the whole. Therefore it will often compel the construction or development of things which end up damaging the individual and the environment and even itself. The brain was created to serve and function as a subordinate organ. Allowed to (or even forced to) function without direction, it becomes as an army without a general.

Become aware of the pattern. Notice how your mind desires to work in conjunction with how your heart feels. Allow yourself to be guided.

Chapter Two

The Heart's Intellectual and Judgmental Abilities:
Linking Quran, Hadith, and Science

« جِئْتَ تَسْأَلُ عَنِ البِرِّ ؟ » قُلْتُ : نَعَمْ. قَالَ :

« اسْتَفْتِ قَلْبَكَ ، البِرُّ مَا اطْمَأَنَّتْ إِلَيْهِ النَّفْسُ

وَاطْمَأَنَّ إِلَيْهِ القَلْبُ ، وَالإِثْمُ مَا حَاكَ فِي النَّفْسِ

وَتَرَدَّدَ فِي الصَّدْرِ وَإِنْ أَفْتَاكَ النَّاسُ وَأَفْتَوْكَ » .

The Prophet (saw) said to a man who approached him, "You have come to ask me about righteousness? Consult your heart. Righteousness is that about which the soul feels tranquil and the heart feels tranquil and wrongdoing is that which waivers in the soul and moves back and forth in the chest even though people have again and again given you an opinion supporting it."
(An-Nawawi's Forty Hadith #27)

This quote from Muhammad Ibn Abdullah (saw), the last prophet of Allah (swt) to all humanity, is more than 1,400 years old. It indicates a wise and currently uncommon knowing of a function of the sound heart. Although today such knowledge is rare among believing men and women, it must have been taught to Adam, as Allah (iwj) says in Quran:

وَعَلَّمَ ءَادَمَ ٱلْأَسْمَآءَ كُلَّهَا ثُمَّ عَرَضَهُمْ عَلَى ٱلْمَلَـٰٓئِكَةِ
فَقَالَ أَنۢبِـُٔونِى بِأَسْمَآءِ هَـٰٓؤُلَآءِ إِن كُنتُمْ صَـٰدِقِينَ ﴿٣١﴾

"...and He taught Adam the names of all things;
Then He placed them before the Angels and said,
Tell Me the names of these things, if you are truthful." [1]

This knowledge was passed on to humanity through the children of Adam (as) and has resurfaced at various times throughout history in the wise teachings of many. It is now being restated in various ways by the modern "spiritual gurus" or guides to self-empowerment, personal growth and fulfillment. Deepak Chopra, in his popular "Seven Spiritual Laws to Success" says:

"The heart is intuitive, it's holistic, it's contextual, it's relational ... It taps into the cosmic computer and takes everything into account ... the heart has a computing ability that is far more accurate and far more precise than anything within the limits of rational thought." [2]

He indicates that sensations in the physical body (in the area of the chest) of comfort or discomfort are part of a universal mechanism to assist us in making right choices. His specific instruction to anyone seeking to make the right choice is, "Consciously put your attention in the heart and ask your heart what to do. ... Only the heart knows the correct answer." [3] Iyanla Van Zandt, another of these "guides" directs those who come to her for guidance to "Disconnect your brain. Now breathe (through the heart)." [4] She then elicits the answers to life's queries, which seem to float up and out, though previously inaccessible. These two, and a host of others, have grabbed the attention of tens of thousands of adherents by merely reiterating and rewriting advice that the Muslim community has had for over a millennium − Istafti-l-qalb (Consult the heart).

In the Quran, when our creation is succinctly described, Allah (swt) says:

"And Allah has brought you out of the wombs of your mothers; you knew nothing; and He endowed you with the faculties of hearing, and seeing and feeling and intellect so that you might show gratitude." [5]

Allah (swt) redirects our attention several times in subsequent

Surahs

to these three important faculties with which we are blessed. Ayat 26 of Surah Ahqaf (46) and ayat of Surat ul Mulk (67) repeat the Arabic words of sam'a, absara, and af'idat (hearing, seeing and feeling/intellect respectively). Respected translator and commentator of the Quran, Yusuf Ali, says in his footnotes of Surah Al-Ahqaf,

Errata Sheet

Pages 36-37

THE MAGNIFICENT ORGAN

The Heart of Quran, Hadith,
Science, and Wholistic
Healing Experiences

Allah (swt) redirects our attention several times in subsequent Surahs to these three important faculties with which we are blessed. Ayat 26 of Surah Ahqaf (46) and ayat of Surah ul-Mulk (67) repeat the Arabic words of sam'a, absara, and af'idat (hearing, seeing, and feeling/intellect respectfully). Respected translator and commentator of the Quran, Yusuf Ali, says in his footnotes of Surat Al-Ahqaf,

> *Hearing and seeing refer to the experimental faculties; the word "heart" in Arabic includes intellect, or the rational faculties as well as the instruments of feeling and emotion, the aesthetic faculties."* [6]

intellect, or the rational faculties as well as the instruments of feeling and emotion, the aesthetic faculties. " [6]

Clarifying the Terminology:

It is, at this point, of importance to note and thoroughly understand the three Arabic terms used by Allah (swt) in Quran and the Prophet Muhammad (saw) to refer to the heart and its faculties. These three - Qalb and its plural Quloob; sadr and its plural sudoor; and fu'ad and its plural af'idat – are interchangeably used to refer to the heart, depending on the context.

The first of these, Qalb, is derived from the root word (verb) qa la ba, which means to turn, turn side to side, upside down or around. It is the main term used to refer to the actual flesh organ (mudghat). The significance of its root word is in the fact that the heart is set by Allah (iwj) in a direction (fitrah) of purity and truth but can be turned away and corrupted and also turned back to its original state. The word Sadr is literally the location of the qalb, the physical cavity or chest, the "holy seat."

37

Allah (swt) says in Quran: "Surely it is not the eyes that are blind but certainly the blindness is of the hearts which are in the chests." [7] Even so, the sadr (or sudoor) is also at times translated as hearts (centers of feeling). [8] The final term is fu'ad. This is used most often for feelings, emotions but also implies, as stated earlier, intellect. [9]

The faculties described by these terms, and emphasized to us by The All Knowing and Wise, are means by which we can acquire knowledge, both from the finite and infinite worlds. We then use that collected information to form judgments, make decisions and choices, guide our thoughts and actions and thereby cultivate our character and our destiny. The use of these faculties, combined with our predisposed (from DNA) personalities, ultimately determine who we are. Being conscious of such a magnificent gift requires an exchange of gratitude and careful attention to how the faculties are used. Admonition is given for those who fail in this respect.

Allah (swt) has additionally mentioned that these faculties can be expanded by His grace[10] and stimulated by travel and observation:

أَفَلَمْ يَسِيرُوا۟ فِى ٱلْأَرْضِ
فَتَكُونَ لَهُمْ قُلُوبٌ يَعْقِلُونَ بِهَآ أَوْ ءَاذَانٌ يَسْمَعُونَ بِهَآ فَإِنَّهَا
لَا تَعْمَى ٱلْأَبْصَٰرُ وَلَٰكِن تَعْمَى ٱلْقُلُوبُ ٱلَّتِى فِى ٱلصُّدُورِ ۝

"Do they not travel through the earth so that their heart can gain wisdom and their ears can learn to hear?"[11]

In this verse it is particularly indicated that intelligence ('aqul) is a function of the heart. This is of stunning significance in light of the fact that scientists have recently discovered these amazing "new" (knowledge is as old as Adam) facts about the heart: (a) The heart thinks; (b) The cells of the heart have a coded memory; (c) Both of the above processes are related to a subtle energy with unverified properties.[12] Science and not metaphysics is now teaching that the heart has an intellect and wisdom. The suggestion is that it has gone unnoticed heretofore because of its subtle and gentle nature in contrast with the brain's assertive and demanding one.

39

That the heart has a knowing ability is undeniable. Also, reflective, contemplative consideration of Quranic ayah will cause one to understand that the function of the heart far exceeds sustaining the life and health of the physical body.

Quranic Verification of Multi-faceted Action of the Heart:

Often knowledge is symbolically represented by light and wisdom is its enhancement or embellisher. In Quran, Allah (iwj) is referred to as "the light of the heavens and the earth"[13] and this light is described as "light upon light"; depths and layers that will never be completely perceived by the human being. Yet, we are continually given glimpses and allowed flashes, which illuminate our darkness and replace veils or spots of ignorance with knowledge (light). If we are truly blessed, Allah (swt) may even embellish that knowledge with understanding and wisdom. We pray for such a blessing.

The first mention in Quran of any of the three key words given earlier is "qalb" (heart), which appears early in Surah-tul Baqarah. It appears in its plural form, quloob, as Allah (iwj) speaks about those who reject truth, "alladheena kafaroo" saying:

إِنَّ ٱلَّذِينَ كَفَرُواْ سَوَآءٌ عَلَيْهِمْ ءَأَنذَرْتَهُمْ أَمْ لَمْ تُنذِرْهُمْ لَا يُؤْمِنُونَ ۝ خَتَمَ ٱللَّهُ عَلَىٰ قُلُوبِهِمْ وَعَلَىٰ سَمْعِهِمْ وَعَلَىٰٓ أَبْصَـٰرِهِمْ غِشَـٰوَةٌ وَلَهُمْ عَذَابٌ عَظِيمٌ ۝

"Surely for those who have rejected faith, it is the same whether you warn them or you don't warn them. Allah has sealed their hearts, and their hearing and on their vision is a veil. And for them is a terrible punishment." [14]

Obviously, this does not mean that Allah causes their hearts to stop beating or pumping blood because such people usually continue on in their physical lives. But, it does indicate that some aspect of the heart's ability has been cut off or sealed. When you consider this Ayat with the wisdom of the hadith of the Prophet Muhammad (saw) that began this chapter, it becomes clear that the

41

heart has some ability to discern right from wrong, to make judgments and communicate that information to our conscious minds. This conclusion can be supported by the existence of neurotransmitters in both the brain and the heart and the electrochemical information that passes between them. But, additionally, one can conclude that the heart is receptive to and communicates more than physical information. In Quran, Allah ta'alaa states that revelation descended on the heart of Prophet Muhammad (saw):

قُلْ

مَن كَانَ عَدُوًّا لِجِبْرِيلَ فَإِنَّهُۥ نَزَّلَهُۥ عَلَىٰ قَلْبِكَ بِإِذْنِ ٱللَّهِ مُصَدِّقًا لِّمَا بَيْنَ يَدَيْهِ وَهُدًى وَبُشْرَىٰ لِلْمُؤْمِنِينَ

۞

"And surely he brought it down to your heart by Allah's permission." [15]

This important fact is later restated.

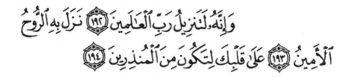

"Surely this is a revelation of the Lord of the worlds. He sent it down with the trustworthy spirit (Jibreel/Gabriel) to your heart that you might be one of the warners." (16)

Revelation direct from the Creator via the angels is sent to the heart. From there it becomes part of conscious knowledge. How? The heart communicates that knowledge to the brain. As a commentary on the translation of the Arabic word "qalb" in the above quote from Surah Shu'araa, Yusuf Ali states, "qalb (heart) signifies not only the seat of the affections but also the seat of the memory and understanding." (17) Allah t'alaa reveals to the heart and sends the Prophets to give us instruction. The Prophet(saw) says, "consult the heart" because there lies recorded information of wisdom and guidance that we can access for personal and communal benefit.

Recorded information? Absolutely! Since the early 1980's, Allah has allowed the scientific community to know how atoms, cells and organs store coded information.[18] For various reasons, including the fear of being ridiculed, that information was not made public until 1993. Today it is common knowledge in certain circles. It is, therefore, verifiable that the heart is entrusted with storing various types of information and that we are meant and even instructed to access and make use of it. The Heart knows all revealed universal truths and in its normal functioning will guide us by them. It is also governed by universal laws. One of these laws is the Law of Gratitude,

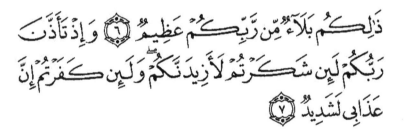

"If you are grateful, I will grant you an increase. But if you are ungrateful, surely my punishment is terrible indeed." [19]

There are natural rewards and consequences established in the universe. I remember a Professor of Nutrition at the University of Missouri saying many years ago, "You do not break the laws of the universe. They will break you." Ingratitude for the intellect and guidance of the heart shown by conscious and arrogant rejection, argumentative disputing, or indulgence of one's own base desires while disregarding the guidance provided, results in a "sealing," a natural cutting off of particular abilities of the heart.

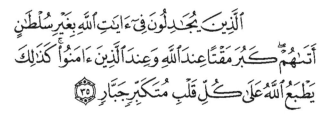

"Those who dispute about the signs of Allah without any authority having been given to them, grievous and odious is it (such conduct) in the sight of Allah and the believers. So it is that Allah seals every heart of the arrogant and obstinate ones." [20]

And also,

45

أَفَرَءَيْتَ مَنِ ٱتَّخَذَ إِلَـٰهَهُۥ هَوَىٰهُ وَأَضَلَّهُ ٱللَّهُ عَلَىٰ عِلْمٍ وَخَتَمَ عَلَىٰ سَمْعِهِۦ
وَقَلْبِهِۦ وَجَعَلَ عَلَىٰ بَصَرِهِۦ غِشَـٰوَةً فَمَن يَهْدِيهِ مِنۢ بَعْدِ ٱللَّهِ أَفَلَا
تَذَكَّرُونَ ﴿٢٣﴾

"Do you see the one who takes his desires as his
god? Allah, knowing him as such(a one), has left
him astray and has sealed his hearing and his
heart (and understanding), and has put a cover
over his vision. Then who will guide him, other
than Allah? Will you not, then, be warned?" [21]

Without the proper functioning of perceptive faculties, one

will have a false and distorted perception of reality. What is then

discerned and understood as real and true is not true at all. Truth,

reality, and beauty will only reveal themselves to those who will

accept and appreciate them in this world. Truth in the akhirah (next

life) will be manifested to all. For those who reject and cover truth,

both the primary truth of the existence of a Supreme Creator and

the secondary truths of revelation, prophethood, accountability,

etc., Allah (swt) says He seals the hearts, and the hearing and places

a cover over their vision (see note #14 above). The heart will still

function physically but its deeper, greater capacity to provide spiritual, conscientious guidance is gone. A physical incapacitation then is inevitable, and this is a basic understanding in the wholistic fields as well as with those who explain health from the concept of physics.[22] From an electrical perspective consider that if the reversal of an energy flow from the negative (heart) to the positive (brain) is strong enough, it will short out the negative pole, resulting in a malfunction. The heart is the most powerful muscle in the body, but it can be strained by the increased pressure of a dominating brain and a rebellious spirit. The brain can and has developed ways to correct the physical damage done to the heart – bypass surgery, catheterization, transplants, etc. However, it cannot reverse or bypass the consequences imposed on the heart by the Creator. Moreover, it is not only that the heart can no longer give proper direction, but the receptors of information (the eyes and ears) can no longer function properly in their role related to the physical realm. The deteriorating individual, however, is oblivious.[23] This sealing of perception and capability of human faculties is a natural process which Allah has installed or built into the human fitrah (pattern of creation). It is activated by free will choices. If the wrong choices are consistently made, the consequential outcome is determined. The unrepentant human being is destined for a clearly defined punishment.

To give an example of this concept I will share with you the story of a client with whom I experienced a release of blocked heart energy. This is an example of a self-imposed seal, not a divinely imposed one but, nevertheless, it will help to illuminate the concept.

In the first half of 1997, I was in and out of Chicago, Illinois providing health treatments for a few clients. In the process of treating a young Arab woman with Reflexology, I pressed the heart point on her left foot. She jerked slightly and said, "Ooh, that hurts." I then kept my left hand on the foot point while placing my right hand in the energy field above her heart. An electrical energy surged through me so powerfully it created a noticeable and uncontrollable vibration in my body. When I informed her of what was happening, she said she had noticed some discomfort in the heart area. She then related to me that she had been emotionally shocked and saddened by the attitude of her parents in their response to her stated desire to marry an African-American man. As a result, she had closed off a large portion of her heart energy so she would not feel the pain of this unveiling of her parents' prejudice, nor have to examine its meaning in her life. If this blocking had continued, I am convinced there would have been some form of heart related illness (though there is no way to predict how long it would have taken to clinically manifest) as well as a certain minimal impairment in her ability to recognize future truths. Her inability to handle such an unpleasant truth was increased because of the heart ties between herself and her parents. The heart thrives on joy and love and dislikes pain. However, another essential element of a healthy heart is truth. Any rejection of truth will impede, to some degree, its ability to function.

Chapter 3

The Brain Centered Society

"There are two questions that the thinking heart might ask about the new millennium. It may wonder if we can survive the world our brain has created for us and the pace at which it is running us and, even if the brain is clever enough to keep us alive in its new millennium world, will we want to live in that world if we only end up feeling more disconnected, hostile, self-protective, afraid and alone in the universe – brilliant minds lacking loving souls." **Dr. Paul Pearsall**

Considering the "brain centered" characteristic of western society and the increase in heart diseases, one could embark on another journey of reflective analysis. My personal conclusion is that one cannot naturally avoid thinking with the heart. It is only a deliberate, conscious, and forceful effort that will change the center of one's thought from the heart to the head. It seems logical then that too much of this re-centering may be an additional cause of heart attack and other heart diseases because of the interruption in the natural energy flow.

For several decades the American Medical Association (AMA) has been particularly concerned with the high rate of heart disease. Extensive research has been done and initial blame was placed on sedentary lifestyles and poor eating habits. Those labeled at high risk for heart disease were (and still are) victims of obesity, high cholesterol and high blood pressure as well as those addicted to smoking. Then the factor of stress was introduced; the demanding, fast paced lifestyles partnered with new complexities of technological advancement. This produced the Type A individual - rushing, impatient, short fused, etc. Study after study was made public, dietary changes and exercise regimens were recommended but there are other extremely important facts that were never brought to the public's attention. Statistics showed: (a) that 50% of those suffering a first heart attack had none of the "risk factors"; (b) 80% of those with the "risk factors" never suffered a heart attack.[1] Moreover, an honest evaluation of research done on victims of heart attack would lead one to move outside of the limited cause choices because most victims do not have the qualifying "risk factors." So what, then, are other determinants of heart disease and heart attack? Several reasons can be considered and all have rational validity.

Social Isolation

A lack of supportive family and community, which can be described as broken or fragmented heart ties, has been seriously suggested by researched conclusions as a factor in heart disease. In the 1930's a group of immigrants from northern Italy populated the town of Roseto, Pennsylvania. This community became of interest to researchers when it was found they had lower than expected rates of heart disease even though they did have the identified "risk factors" (high calorie, high cholesterol diet) and were habitual smokers. The second generation, however, which also had the same diet, etc. had heart disease rates similar to the rest of the society.[2] The difference in the two groups was that the younger families had become more isolated and nuclear, functioning as independent units rather than as part of the larger group. They had, in order to join the society, moved away from the joined hearts of family and community. The heart, remember, is integrative. It seeks to join with other hearts and join with the greater whole. It thrives on love, joy and connectedness. Islamically, it remains true to its fitrah as long as possible. Its innate intelligence directs it to perform its task of connection. When it is functioning naturally, it resonates with joy and the sign of that is a steady, regular beat. These smooth, even rhythms have been charted at the Institute of Heart Math and are described as "cardiovascular efficiency" because the heart-brain neurosystem is in harmony. The charted patterns indicate that the heart has achieved synchronicity in its own habitat and resumed its connection with other living systems.

As Muslims we are instructed by Allah (swt) to be "ummatun wahidatun" (one community) joined, in the words of the Prophet (saw), "like bricks in a building." We are to support, encourage and provide for each other's needs. Allah (swt) says:

مُّحَمَّدٌ رَّسُولُ ٱللَّهِ وَٱلَّذِينَ مَعَهُۥٓ أَشِدَّآءُ عَلَى ٱلْكُفَّارِ رُحَمَآءُ بَيْنَهُمْ تَرَىٰهُمْ رُكَّعًا سُجَّدًا يَبْتَغُونَ فَضْلًا مِّنَ ٱللَّهِ وَرِضْوَٰنًا

"Muhammad is the messenger of Allah. And those who are with him are strong against the unbelievers, compassionate amongst each other. You will see them bow and prostrate themselves seeking Grace from Allah and His pleasure." [3]

and also:

كَانُوٓا أَنفُسَهُمْ يَظْلِمُونَ ۝ وَٱلْمُؤْمِنُونَ وَٱلْمُؤْمِنَٰتُ بَعْضُهُمْ أَوْلِيَآءُ بَعْضٍ يَأْمُرُونَ بِٱلْمَعْرُوفِ وَيَنْهَوْنَ عَنِ ٱلْمُنكَرِ وَيُقِيمُونَ ٱلصَّلَوٰةَ وَيُؤْتُونَ ٱلزَّكَوٰةَ وَيُطِيعُونَ ٱللَّهَ وَرَسُولَهُۥٓ أُوْلَٰٓئِكَ سَيَرْحَمُهُمُ ٱللَّهُ إِنَّ ٱللَّهَ عَزِيزٌ حَكِيمٌ ۝

"The believers, men and women, are protectors of one another; they enjoin what is good and just and forbid what is wrong; they observe prayers, practice charity and obey Allah and his Prophet. These are the ones on whom Allah will pour his Mercy. Surely Allah is Exalted and Wise." [4]

Every Muslim is part of an extended family. Our position and role in this universal family becomes even more important when there are no blood relations to provide for the individual or family. If we are not functioning as brother, sister, aunt, uncle to someone; if we are not joining our hearts in compassion and love, then we are not living properly within this Ummah. We are not supporting the heart of our brother/sister.

An excellent example of what this supportive brotherhood can provide to the health and vitality of individuals is the strength maintained by the companions (male and female) of the Prophet (saw) even under extreme privation, including often having nothing to eat.[5] I found a contemporary affirmation of this from a Native American healer, who said:

> *"Prepare your food and eat it with love. That's the way our traditional people did it... They didn't have much to offer, but when people came it didn't take much to satisfy their hunger because there was a lot of love there."* [6]

Community and brotherhood in Islam require action and not just passive thoughts of family and belonging. Its prerequisites are knowledge and understanding: knowing that we are "banu Adam" (children of Adam), one family; knowing that the same "breath" of

Allah that gave one of us distinctive life, gave all of us distinctive life deserving of respect, etc. We must understand how we are responsible to each other and the mutual benefit that is reaped from kindness, mercy, compassion, and love. We also need to somehow understand the consequences of the opposites on our physical, emotional, environmental, and universal worlds.

Brain Centeredness

Disjointedness and disconnection have not passed over the educational system. It too has become increasingly compartmentalized and secular. Most students are not taught the integration of knowledge and that sad reality increases as one moves into the higher levels of the system. Thus, the specialized Ph.D. is usually more detached from the reality of the unity of knowledge than the high school graduate. Both, however, in this western society, are victims of the removal of the truth of Divine Origin of knowledge and any systemic encouragement to express gratitude for it. Considering the previous text, it should not come as a surprise that there is research suggesting that the number of years spent in formal education is more of a determining factor for heart disease than all the other "risk factors" combined.[7] One can literally be educated right out of their true mind and into their brain.

Understand that, as stated before, we are not defining "mind" as it is commonly understood, that is, as a capacity of the brain, but from the Quranic and newly proposed scientific perspective as being directed and dominated by the heart. Without the heart's input, we end up with a brain-centered and brain-created society, an "intense, complex, fast-paced, often soulless world that contributes to failing hearts." [8] Brain-created economics, brain-created foods, brain created technology, medicine, etc., etc., etc. and an environment that has become life threatening to its inhabitants.

The brain is on "full throttle" seemingly unable to stop or even run out of steam. Many Muslims too have become caught in this intellectual, technological rush. Knowing that we are en-couraged and even commanded to seek knowledge, we have hastened to its revered centers and opened our brains to be filled. In doing so, we have most often become casualties of the system; have accepted the separation of religious and secular matters or heart and brain concerns. Thus, education has become a factor in the prevalence of heart disease in many of our communities also. We have become so concerned with becoming scientifically and technologically advanced that we have neglected the heart and its vital integration.

Often it seems that the "heart" of Islam has atrophied in the chests of the Muslims. The heart of man is indeed the heart of our universe. Although we were the last entity to be created and placed in this physical world, everything has been subjected to us and the universe responds, reacts, remains tranquil or convulses as a result of our thoughts, statements and behavior. A rich Quranic verse that gives proof to this wholistic belief is:

ظَهَرَ ٱلْفَسَادُ فِى ٱلْبَرِّ وَٱلْبَحْرِ بِمَا كَسَبَتْ أَيْدِى ٱلنَّاسِ لِيُذِيقَهُم بَعْضَ ٱلَّذِى عَمِلُوا۟ لَعَلَّهُمْ يَرْجِعُونَ ﴿٤١﴾

"Evil and corruption have appeared on land and sea because of what the hands of men have earned, so that they may taste some of (the results of) their deeds and so that they may turn back (from the wrong)." [9]

Diseases of the heart have spread all over the world and have manifested in physical and environmental conditions. Communities free from the physical manifestations/maladies are studied and analyzed, primarily from the socio-biological perspective. The hope is that some aspects of their health supporting lifestyle may be adopted and yield similar results in other places; that perhaps others may learn how to regain this healthy state.

Disconnected Spirit

Historically, religion is directed to the heart and soul of man; concerned with the condition of the spirit. Islam, the original, innate religion of created things, has as a fundamental reality and essential concept the integrity, soundness, wholeness, and unity of the human creature. The very function of activating Islam in our conscious lives and having faith saves us from existing as fragmented, confused beings. In terms of general human well-being, a distinguished Muslim scholar says, "The three most fundamental concepts in Islam mean safety, wholeness, and integrality." [10] These concepts are iman (faith), Islam (surrender), and taqwa (reverence). Islam, therefore, is meant to provide individual and collective health, harmony, and peace. All of the above aspects of human nature are expected to be expressed in both personal and social dimensions so that we may have health and healthy environments. The universe and all within it remains in a basic harmonious state and is, in fact, preserved from destruction by remaining in a state of Islam (complete and absolute submission to the Creator). Therein is a great lesson for those who reflect. It is only with imposition of the errant human being that universal harmony is interrupted.

One of the best known hadith of the Prophet Muhammad (saw) begins by saying, "Islam is built on five." [11] The first of these things is witnessing that Allah is to Whom all worship, glorification and praise is due. By Allah's words in the Quran, all of creation has a knowledge of this and acts accordingly:

$$\text{﴿٤٢﴾ سُبْحَٰنَهُۥ وَتَعَٰلَىٰ عَمَّا يَقُولُونَ عُلُوًّا كَبِيرًا ﴿٤٣﴾ تُسَبِّحُ لَهُ ٱلسَّمَٰوَٰتُ ٱلسَّبْعُ وَٱلْأَرْضُ وَمَن فِيهِنَّ وَإِن مِّن شَىْءٍ إِلَّا يُسَبِّحُ بِحَمْدِهِۦ وَلَٰكِن لَّا تَفْقَهُونَ تَسْبِيحَهُمْ إِنَّهُۥ كَانَ حَلِيمًا غَفُورًا ﴿٤٤﴾ وَإِذَا قَرَأْتَ}$$

"The seven heavens and the earth and all beings therein give glory to Him (Allah). There is not a thing but glorifies Him with praise and yet you don't understand how they declare His glory. Indeed He is oft-Forbearing, Most Forgiving." [12]

Only two segments of the entire creation, humans and jinn (unseen creatures), have the ability to rebel against the natural order and they take full advantage of that ability. Some declare their own divinity and some deny the existence of any such thing. Most however, have simply drifted into a state of neglect of the spirit by leaving off prayer and worship, which was the delight of the Prophet's heart and is described in hadith as nur (light)[13] for those who perform it regularly and with humility. Similarly, it is described in a current writing as "the access to a Higher Source of Power to illuminate our path." [14]

In eastern medicine there is a system of seven energy centers or chakras which absorb primary energy and send it into the physical body. The highest chakra is at the crown of the head and is said to be associated with the "higher mind, knowing and integration of our spiritual and physical makeup." [15] It governs the pineal gland, which is the true master gland of the body. This center is activated and energized by meditation, prayer, dhikr (remembrance) and contemplation of truth. In my experience as a healing agent, I have found the pineal gland to be malfunctioning in many. Inquiry into the lives of these individuals, by simple conversation, will usually verify the neglect of the spirit. It is a societal malaise of epidemic proportion. The wonder to me is how physical bodies continue to function as well as they do without the spiritual energy. Mine won't. Sometimes the vibration of this center slips to such a low frequency level it can be felt as a hum, but occasionally the chakra is actually spinning backwards (counterclockwise) which means energy is, in fact, leaving the body rather than being taken in.

Towards the end of 1998, while practicing in Indiana, I experienced a pronounced counterclockwise spin in the seventh chakra of a middle aged man. He had multiple physical problems, among which was a "pounding heart," a heart demanding attention. His physician had reacted as expected, requiring a heart catheterizatioon and prescribing medication for the condition. He had not, however, been able to get to the root of the problem since medicine, as primarily practiced, is a brain-centered profession. Not only did the medication not heal the heart, it weakened other areas of the system. I did not have to search for the disconnecting factors, which contributed to his compromised condition. They were of such gravity, weighed so heavily on this man's mind that he offered them willingly . He was a religious, church-going individual, but his professional experiences had caused severe conflicts in his ability to remain integral, united in spirit, mind and body. His heart energy was also low and when the heart meridian (electrical energy line) was cleared, he felt a strong "pulsing" down the arm from the shoulder to the fingertips. That restoration of the flow of energy, however, did not mean a cure. It simply meant that the blocked channel or pathway had been reopened, the connection remade. From this point the individual is required to nurture and support the return to wholeness. Unfortunately, many seek to find an easy solution that does not require more from them than money and minimal physical action (i.e. swallowing a pill).

Several years ago there was a melatonin craze in the natural food supplement industry. Melatonin is the hormone produced naturally by the mysterious pineal gland. This production takes place at night, in the dark, when the body is at rest and presupposes several things: (a) that the individual (as much as possible) leads a normal life–working by day and resting by night; (b) that there will be inner harmony that allows the system to rest. Seeking to manually supply the pineal gland's melatonin and not being willing to stimulate its natural production brings its own set of consequences.

Earlier in this century a well known psychologist, said about a group of mentally ill patients:

> *"... every one of them fell ill because he had lost that which the living religions of every age have given to their followers and none of them has really been healed who did not regain his spiritual outlook."* [16]

Without a return to the spirit, mind, body wholistic living, what will occur is a continuation and exacerbation of what we are already witnessing – shocking manifestations of the heartless, spiritually void nature of man: clinical depression, pollution, abusive relationships, societal violence, rampant immorality and an obsession with material gain, which drives the heart beyond its physiological limits.

The disease penetrates and contaminates every segment of society and would lead to our total destruction except that there remain among us those who believe in Allah (God) and follow the Divine guidance and remember this command:

وَٱصْبِرْ نَفْسَكَ مَعَ ٱلَّذِينَ يَدْعُونَ رَبَّهُم بِٱلْغَدَوٰةِ وَٱلْعَشِيِّ يُرِيدُونَ وَجْهَهُۥ وَلَا تَعْدُ عَيْنَاكَ عَنْهُمْ تُرِيدُ زِينَةَ ٱلْحَيَوٰةِ ٱلدُّنْيَا وَلَا تُطِعْ مَنْ أَغْفَلْنَا قَلْبَهُۥ عَن ذِكْرِنَا وَٱتَّبَعَ هَوَىٰهُ وَكَانَ أَمْرُهُۥ فُرُطًا ﴿٢٨﴾

"Let your heart be content with those who call on their Lord by day and night, desiring to be in His presence and don't obey anyone whose heart we have allowed to neglect our remembrance and who follows his own desires." [17]

Chapter 4

The Heart's Righting Ability

« إِنَّ الْحَلَالَ بَيِّنٌ ، وَإِنَّ الْحَرَامَ بَيِّنٌ ، وَبَيْنَهُمَا
أُمُورٌ مُشْتَبِهَاتٌ لَا يَعْلَمُهُنَّ كَثِيرٌ مِنَ النَّاسِ . فَمَنْ
اتَّقَى الشُّبُهَاتِ فَقَدِ اسْتَبْرَأَ لِدِينِهِ وَعِرْضِهِ . وَمَنْ
وَقَعَ فِي الشُّبُهَاتِ وَقَعَ فِي الْحَرَامِ ، كَالرَّاعِي
يَرْعَى حَوْلَ الْحِمَى يُوشِكُ أَنْ يَرْتَعَ فِيهِ . أَلَا
وَإِنَّ لِكُلِّ مَلِكٍ حِمًى ، أَلَا وَإِنَّ حِمَى اللهِ مَحَارِمُهُ.
أَلَا وَإِنَّ فِي الْجَسَدِ مُضْغَةً، إِذَا صَلَحَتْ صَلَحَ
الْجَسَدُ كُلُّهُ ، وَإِذَا فَسَدَتْ فَسَدَ الْجَسَدُ كُلُّهُ ، أَلَا
وَهِيَ الْقَلْبُ » .

"That which is lawful is plain and that which is unlawful is plain and between the two are doubtful matters about which not many people know. Thus he who avoids doubtful matters clears himself in regard to his religion and his honor. But he who falls into doubtful matters falls into that which is unlawful. (He is) like the shepherd who pastures around a sanctuary all but grazing his flock in it. Indeed every king has a sanctuary, and truly Allah's sanctuary is His prohibitions. Indeed in the body there is a morsel of flesh which if it is right and good, then the whole body is right but if it is corrupted then the whole body is corrupted. Indeed this is the heart." (Hadith of Prophet Muhammad)

From the wording of this hadith (saying), two things are obvious. One, that the heart spoken of is definitely a physical organ and secondly, that the indicated ability to right or corrupt is not limited to a physical nature but related also to morality, virtue, and truth. Implied, or of a not so obvious nature, is the fact that the condition of the physical body (jasad) may be directly related to the decisions made regarding the lawful and unlawful or the right and the wrong. By the wording, the Prophet (saw) has also indicated the authoritative position of the heart; that it takes precedence over other organs regarding the overall condition of the body. Physically it is like other organs in many ways but distinct in its superior abilities. Its physical location in the body is similar to the sun in our solar system. Its material referral in Oriental medicine is fire.[1] It affects the condition of every other system including the immune system, which is responsible for identifying and remembering what is natural and beneficial to the inner environment and what is foreign and threatening. The immune system is our defense system with several lines of defense. The immune cells can "read" the messages sent via electro-magnetic energy and respond accordingly. If harmful substances can not be kept from entering the body by our first line of defense (skin, nose, etc.), then the interior defenders must activate. The heart acts as a director on both levels. It reacts to situations as its energy pushes for and relays info-energy to our system. When the atria contract, the hormone produced connects directly with the hypothalamus in the brain and the pineal gland. This electro-hormonal connection facilitates the immune response, whether it is in reaction to a physical or emotional stimulus. Internally it restricts flow to some areas and increases it to others, allowing the immune system priority as needed. The heart maintains the integrity of the system, allowing each cell to continue to perform according to its programmed code. Externally and internally it will keep a balanced flow of life sustaining fluid or increase and restrict it according to the needs of the system.

> *"Even a simple intention such as metabolizing a molecule of sugar immediately sets off a symphony of events in the body where precise amounts of hormones have to be secreted at precise moments to convert this molecule of sugar into pure creative energy."* [2]

The symphony of physical life could not continue as such without the circulatory system governed by the healthy heart. Conversely, a single episode involving negativity (of thought or action) will upset the balance and disrupt the harmony.

> *"A single episode of anger or even its recall can depress the immune system for almost an entire day."* [3]

Knowing this, a reasonable person can see another level of wisdom in the repeated advice of the Prophet Muhammad (saw), "Do not get angry." [4] Cleansing the heart of negative emotions (hate, anger, resentment, etc.) is not only spiritually uplifting but enhances physical health by enabling the immune system.

Frequently the danger threatening the individual is not physical but spiritual or social/psychological. In these cases the heart's supervision is essential, as the brain is incapable of making moral or wholistic judgments. Dr. Pearsall states that neuro-scientists have yet to find one major central memory center in the brain[5] and memory is essential when judgment is needed. There is a process of association, translation and cognitive awareness that must take place often within split seconds. The Prophet (saw) indicates in one Hadith that piety (taqwa) resides in the chest or heart.

لَا تَحَاسَدُوا ، وَلَا تَنَاجَشُوا،وَلَا تَبَاغَضُوا ،

وَلَا تَدَابَرُوا ، وَلَا يَبِعْ بَعْضُكُمْ عَلَى بَيْعِ بَعْضٍ .

وَكُونُوا ، عِبَادَ اللهِ، إِخْوَاناً. اَلْمُسْلِمُ أَخُو الْمُسْلِمِ :

لَا يَظْلِمُهُ ، وَلَا يَخْذُلُهُ ، وَلَا يَكْذِبُهُ ، وَلَا يَحْقِرُهُ .

التَّقْوَى هُهْنَا ـ وَيُشِيرُ إِلَى صَدْرِهِ ثَلَاثَ مَرَّاتٍ ـ

بِحَسْبِ امْرِئٍ مِنَ الشَّرِّ أَنْ يَحْقِرَ أَخَاهُ الْمُسْلِمَ .

كُلُّ الْمُسْلِمِ عَلَى الْمُسْلِمِ حَرَامٌ : دَمُهُ ، وَمَالُهُ ،

وَعِرْضُهُ » .

"... Be you, Oh servants of Allah, brothers. A Muslim is the brother of a Muslim. He neither lies to him nor does he hold him in contempt. Piety is right here (and he pointed to his chest three times)." [6]

The Arabic word "taqwa" is often translated as fear of Allah but also as consciousness or awareness. A consciousness emanating from the heart is so perfect because it has memory of its primal origin, awareness of the universe and a life memory.

The latter has been documented, studied and reported in biographical and scientific texts. Evidence now shows that the heart is the repository of a person's life memories. Much of the information about a phenomenal heart memory, capable of influencing and modifying desires, speech and behavior has been obtained from heart transplant recipients.[7] With the transplant of the physical organ, these individuals also have received the memories, preferences, and personality traits of their donors. The recent scientific and medical discoveries in this area are compatible with Divine knowledge contained in Quran and Hadith. The Ayurvedic system, an ancient healing system originating in India, also teaches that there is systemic knowledge – that the body will guide you and tell you what (exercise, food, rest, etc.) it needs and in what quantity. From where does this knowing originate and how is it communicated to the conscious mind?

The Corrupted Heart

There is an old legend that says,

"God, at the beginning of time, with the objective of populating the earth, created many beings at one time and distributed amongst them various qualities. He gave good judgment to the Greeks, manual ingenuity to the Chinese and superiority of language to the Arabs." [8]

The Arabic vocabulary is best at expressing concepts and explaining characteristics of things. As previously stated, the root of the word qalb, which signifies the heart, means to turn. The heart turns naturally to its Creator but can be turned away or corrupted. Kufr, rejection of a Divine presence and rejection of truth and guidance will weaken the heart, leaving it vulnerable to all types of corruption and disease.

But, even in its prenatal existence, the heart may be compromised and weakened. Many factors – maternal, environmental, nutritional, etc. – will begin to determine its level of soundness and health. A heart that thrives on spiritual communication, love, joy, peace and all things of good will sicken from the opposite. There is a Japanese concept called

Tai Kyo, which teaches that voices, thoughts, and feelings of the family members will influence the fetus. Therefore, the pregnant woman must avoid disharmonious encounters of all kinds. One teacher of this way relates,

> *"Improper diet, loud sounds, disharmonious thoughts and wild erratic behavior or lifestyle can have a tremendous impact on the person's entire future mental, physical and spiritual constitution and development."* [9]

As the individual matures, the heart continues to be influenced by its physical and spiritual environment. Signs of the troubled heart are alternating conditions of sickness and health. There will be the desire for right and wrong, for good, healthy food and unhealthy food, for virtuous companions and decadent ones, etc. Choices will be made according to which influence is dominant at any given time. Once an individual reaches an age of accountability and negative choices are made, the heart is weakened slightly. Repeated negative indulgences will eventually destroy the heart's ability to turn back to righteousness and health. Such a person will have stripped themselves of the protective and healing nature of the heart.

The Seeds of Weakness

Since the heart is our link between the physical and spiritual, its health is sustained by proper nourishment in both of these realms. The heart will be physically compromised by **excessive eating** and consumption of haram (forbidden) foods. The one who eats slowly showing respect for the food and does not overeat, will find that he enjoys the food more and that the heart will be peaceful. This is because there will be no feeling of shame or guilt for having exceeded the limits of moderation and because the food will be better digested and assimilated. Excessive eating will result in the opposite of this condition meaning that there will be poor digestion and assimilation and the heart will be disturbed. Also, the Prophet (saw) has said:

> *"The believer eats in one intestine and is satisfied with a little food, while the kafir (one who rejects faith) eats in seven intestines."* [10]

Indulgence of temptations is another cause of a weakened heart. Every individual is created good, with a decent, pure nature that

77

loves righteousness and detests wickedness and evil. While remaining in this state, if it indulges in wrong of any kind, it feels sad and remorseful. However, every individual also has the capacity to be attracted to or excited by glamorized indecency and sinful acts.[11] Every sinful thought, word or deed indulged will leave a stain on the heart and character. Continual indulgence, without repentance and seeking of forgiveness, darkens the heart and ruins the character. Obstinate opposition to Allah t'alaa is an illness that proves fatal to the nafs (natural personality).[12]

Temptations are on all levels and to every human stage. The child may be tempted to disobey the parent and view a prohibited television show. The teenager may be tempted to overrule his/her sense of right and steal a desired item. The adult may be tempted to indulge a forbidden sexual inclination. Dwelling on the wrong will blur the barrier between good and evil and create confusion in reasoning. Shaitan (Satan) will enter to support the wrong and encourage us to allow our desires to dominate.

وَمَن يَعْشُ عَن ذِكْرِ ٱلرَّحْمَٰنِ نُقَيِّضْ لَهُۥ شَيْطَٰنًا
فَهُوَ لَهُۥ قَرِينٌ ۝ وَإِنَّهُمْ لَيَصُدُّونَهُمْ عَنِ ٱلسَّبِيلِ وَيَحْسَبُونَ
أَنَّهُم مُّهْتَدُونَ ۝

"If anyone forsakes the remembrance of the Most Gracious, we appoint for him a devil, then he (that devil) becomes for him a companion. Surely, they will hinder them from the Path, yet they think they are being guided rightly." [13]

In the late nineteenth century, a pioneer of internal medicine wrote that atherosclerosis (hardening and clogging of arterial passages) is "the Nemesis through which nature exacts retributional justice for transgressions of her laws." [14] He described patients with this condition as having aggressive worldly ambitions (brain driven). Self indulgence is a facet of the selfish, ego-centered personality, which leads to hardness of the heart.

The tongue, created to be servant of the righteous heart, can also be an agent of destruction. In both Christian and Muslim traditions it is known as a key to heaven or hell. Our gift of speech has the ability to lift us to great heights or cast us down into the depths of indecency. The heart will grow weary from participation in **unnecessary and foolish talking**. Called laghwun in Arabic, it is that talk which serves no purpose of good and is just a waste of time and breath. It is mentioned several times in Quran as being distasteful and destructive.[15] Allah (swt) wants to impress upon us its repugnancy and so mentions specifically that inhabitants of the paradise will be protected from it.

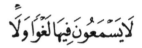

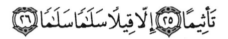

"There, they will not hear any foolishness nor any sinful talk, only the saying of "Peace, Peace." [16]

Following a general pattern, deviation from the good and virtuous behavior leads to gradual degeneration. Frivolous talk, not abandoned, will eventually lead to quarrels, obscenities, lies, etc. And the Prophet (saw) has said,

> *"When a man gets up in the morning, all the limbs humble themselves before the tongue and say, 'Fear Allah for our sake, for we are dependent on you. If you are straight, we are straight. But if you are crooked, then we are crooked."* [17]

I would like to mention two more things that will cause the heart to lose its ability to keep the system and self healthy and whole. They are **failure to restrain the eyes and keeping of bad company**. First, related to the eyes, they are the most complex nervous unit operating in the body and there is an immediate and direct connection between the eye and the heart. A large part of the cerebral cortex located at the back of the head is related to vision. It is concerned with processing information from the retina and relaying that information to the heart so that the heart can direct the system accordingly. Hardening of the heart or a desensitizing of its compassion can be effected by repeated viewing of violent acts, as so painfully evidenced by the recent shocking behavior of some American youth. Lack of judgment and inclination to immorality is also a fault of the unrestrained eye by rejecting the guidance of Allah.

قُل لِّلْمُؤْمِنِينَ يَغُضُّوا مِنْ أَبْصَارِهِمْ وَيَحْفَظُوا فُرُوجَهُمْ
ذَٰلِكَ أَزْكَىٰ لَهُمْ إِنَّ ٱللَّهَ خَبِيرٌۢ بِمَا يَصْنَعُونَ ﴿٣٠﴾ وَقُل لِّلْمُؤْمِنَـٰتِ
يَغْضُضْنَ مِنْ أَبْصَارِهِنَّ وَيَحْفَظْنَ فُرُوجَهُنَّ وَلَا يُبْدِينَ
زِينَتَهُنَّ إِلَّا مَا ظَهَرَ مِنْهَا ۖ وَلْيَضْرِبْنَ بِخُمُرِهِنَّ عَلَىٰ جُيُوبِهِنَّ ۖ
وَلَا يُبْدِينَ زِينَتَهُنَّ إِلَّا لِبُعُولَتِهِنَّ أَوْ ءَابَآئِهِنَّ أَوْ
ءَابَآءِ بُعُولَتِهِنَّ أَوْ أَبْنَآئِهِنَّ أَوْ أَبْنَآءِ بُعُولَتِهِنَّ
أَوْ إِخْوَٰنِهِنَّ أَوْ بَنِىٓ إِخْوَٰنِهِنَّ أَوْ بَنِىٓ أَخَوَٰتِهِنَّ أَوْ نِسَآئِهِنَّ
أَوْ مَا مَلَكَتْ أَيْمَـٰنُهُنَّ أَوِ ٱلتَّـٰبِعِينَ غَيْرِ أُو۟لِى ٱلْإِرْبَةِ مِنَ
ٱلرِّجَالِ أَوِ ٱلطِّفْلِ ٱلَّذِينَ لَمْ يَظْهَرُوا عَلَىٰ عَوْرَٰتِ ٱلنِّسَآءِ ۖ
وَلَا يَضْرِبْنَ بِأَرْجُلِهِنَّ لِيُعْلَمَ مَا يُخْفِينَ مِن زِينَتِهِنَّ ۚ وَتُوبُوٓا
إِلَى ٱللَّهِ جَمِيعًا أَيُّهَ ٱلْمُؤْمِنُونَ لَعَلَّكُمْ تُفْلِحُونَ ﴿٣١﴾

"And say to the believing men to lower their gaze and protect their modesty; that is purer for them... Surely Allah is well aware of what they do. And say to the believing women to lower their gaze and guard their modesty ..." [18]

The eyes must be used to serve the heart and the spirit. Used improperly, they will render the heart blind to the distinction between truth and falsehood. A sustained diet of negative visual images will desensitize the automatic voice of conscience emanating from the heart.

Finally, we must briefly consider the selection of companions and how this effects the heart. I say briefly because Chapter Six will go into this aspect with some detail. The law of "opposites attract" applies in almost every level of creation except within the human species. In our personal connections it is "like attracts like" that is the operating energetic law. Every human being creates an energy field, which surrounds them, composed of the vibrations of thoughts, feelings, beliefs, and completed actions. Others are either drawn to or repulsed by that vibrational field. At all levels of conscious function we utilize our freedom of choice, though not always with equal strength. When anyone chooses to associate with another person or group with undesirable characteristics, they have chosen to expose themselves to negative influences. Continued exposure to the negative energy will eventually bring changes in the character just as water can gradually shape rock and earth. The individual may not see it happening but others will notice the change.

Human beings are joined by ties of the heart, whether it be to a blood relative or a chosen friend. We cannot help unplanned encounters and imposed situations such as spending time with co-workers or immoral family members. Even so, our Creator has advised,

يَٰٓأَيُّهَا ٱلَّذِينَ ءَامَنُوا۟ لَا تَتَّخِذُوٓا۟ ءَابَآءَكُمْ وَإِخْوَٰنَكُمْ أَوْلِيَآءَ إِنِ ٱسْتَحَبُّوا۟ ٱلْكُفْرَ عَلَى ٱلْإِيمَٰنِ وَمَن يَتَوَلَّهُم مِّنكُمْ فَأُو۟لَٰٓئِكَ هُمُ ٱلظَّٰلِمُونَ ﴿٢٣﴾

"Oh you who believe, don't take your fathers and brothers as close friends and protectors, if they love unfaithfulness above faith. If any of you do so, you do wrong." [19]

and

يَٰٓأَيُّهَا ٱلَّذِينَ ءَامَنُوا۟ لَا تَتَّخِذُوا۟ ٱلَّذِينَ ٱتَّخَذُوا۟ دِينَكُمْ هُزُوًا وَلَعِبًا مِّنَ ٱلَّذِينَ أُوتُوا۟ ٱلْكِتَٰبَ مِن قَبْلِكُمْ وَٱلْكُفَّارَ أَوْلِيَآءَ وَٱتَّقُوا۟ ٱللَّهَ إِن كُنتُم مُّؤْمِنِينَ ﴿٥٧﴾

"Oh you who believe take not for friends and protectors those who take your religion for a mockery or sport – whether among those who received the Scriptures before you or among those who reject faith. But have reverence for Allah, if you are believers." [20]

Remaining in the company of such people or seeking them out for association, advice or assistance is a poison to the heart. It interferes with its electro-magnetic field and weakens its power of discernment by causing it to disobey its Creator (swt). The proven axiom of psycho-social science will definitely be operating – "Association brings assimilation".

The Healthy Heart

As the Prophet Muhammad (saw) has conveyed, the condition of the body will reflect the condition of the heart. A chief concern in today's societies, especially those of the West, is how to sustain heart health. First, it must be acknowledged that the heart is more than a physical muscle, a lump of flesh or a cluster of specialized cells. The heart is the most mystical, spiritual organ in existence and its preferred sustenance is of a spiritual nature – the ecstasy of knowing its Lord, the enjoyment of worshipping and the delight drawn from acts done exclusively for the pleasure of the Creator and the experience of love. Allah (swt) has revealed verses to make us aware of the needs of the heart.

For example,

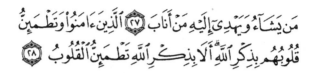

"Those who believe and whose hearts find contentment in the remembrance of Allah. For isn't it in the remembrance of Allah that the hearts do find contentment?" [21]

The heart is made peaceful with prayer, contemplation, and gratitude. Science is giving confirmation to Allah's words by showing that the accelerated heart rate and nervous anxiety caused by the fast-paced life of this technological, materially demanding world can be alleviated by meditation, biofeedback, and prayer. Yes, the medical profession is now even admitting the benefits of prayer on the health of the human body. The contentment and peace of the heart is also partially dependent upon satisfaction of its need to know and understand some workings of the universe as is indicated by the curiosity of Prophet Ibraheem (as) as he beseeched Allah (swt):

وَإِذْ قَالَ إِبْرَاهِيمُ رَبِّ أَرِنِي كَيْفَ تُحْيِ الْمَوْتَى قَالَ أَوَلَمْ تُؤْمِنْ قَالَ بَلَى وَلَكِن لِّيَطْمَئِنَّ قَلْبِي

"My Lord, show me how you give life to the dead. He (Allah) said, 'Is it that you don't believe?' Of course, it is only a need to satisfy my heart." [22]

The need of the heart to reverently remember its Only Lord and understand, with its limited capacity, how life functions is rooted in the purpose of creation. The knowledge of the primal purpose is seeded in the heart's code and only needs to be "watered" from time to time. Our curiosities about our own purpose, about the function and meaning of life and about what is meaningful and worthy of our focused energies are necessary in order to keep us seeking the truth, which resides in the hearts. In Quran, Allah ta'alaa has indicated three main reasons for the human creation:

"I only created humans and jinn that they might worship Me." [23]

وَإِذۡ قَالَ رَبُّكَ لِلۡمَلَـٰٓئِكَةِ إِنِّى جَاعِلٌ فِى ٱلۡأَرۡضِ خَلِيفَةࣰ

"And as your Lord said to the angels, Surely, I will create a vicegerent on the earth." [(24)]

وَجَٰهِدُوا۟ فِى ٱللَّهِ حَقَّ جِهَادِهِۦۚ هُوَ ٱجۡتَبَىٰكُمۡ وَمَا جَعَلَ عَلَيۡكُمۡ فِى ٱلدِّينِ مِنۡ حَرَجࣲۚ مِّلَّةَ أَبِيكُمۡ إِبۡرَٰهِيمَۚ هُوَ سَمَّىٰكُمُ ٱلۡمُسۡلِمِينَ مِن قَبۡلُ وَفِى هَـٰذَا لِيَكُونَ ٱلرَّسُولُ شَهِيدًا عَلَيۡكُمۡ وَتَكُونُوا۟ شُهَدَآءَ عَلَى ٱلنَّاسِۚ فَأَقِيمُوا۟ ٱلصَّلَوٰةَ وَءَاتُوا۟ ٱلزَّكَوٰةَ وَٱعۡتَصِمُوا۟ بِٱللَّهِ هُوَ مَوۡلَىٰكُمۡۖ فَنِعۡمَ ٱلۡمَوۡلَىٰ وَنِعۡمَ ٱلنَّصِيرُ ۝

"He has named you Muslims before and in this revelation so that the Messenger may be a witness for you and you can be witnesses for humanity. So establish prayer and give zakat (charity) and hold fast to Allah. He is your Protector and an excellent Protector and an excellent Helper." [(25)]

a) to worship of Allah, b) to maintain his creation, c) to be witnesses (to be the best examples) for humanity.

Healthy hearts are dependent upon **worship of Allah, maintenance of the creation and leading exemplary lives** according to divine laws and principles. The Quran properly followed will render the heart healthy. Divine laws are

88

followed will render the heart healthy. Divine laws are prescribed for soundness and peace of the individual as well as for health and wholeness of societies. The most fundamental law restated in every prophetic message is that the Lord, God is One and that you should not worship anything or anyone else along with your Lord. It is clearly found in the Torah, Bible, and Quran. Turning the heart away from this innate, essential knowledge will instigate a diseased condition. As it creates anxiety and restlessness, the immune system response will become impaired and any variety of diseases can result.

According to dated Islamic writings, all roots of goodness reside in the healthy heart and can bloom as required.[26] This heart is described as " qalbun saleemun" or a heart at peace. (Here it is helpful to refer back to Chapter One's reference to the smooth rhythms of cardio-vascular efficiency). The outstanding characteristic of such a heart is that it is attracted to what is good and pure including behavior, associates, and items of physical nourishment. It will feel discomfort with and repulse impure and self-development before arriving at the position of the heart described above. Choices must be made at every level, engaging the unique property given to humans and jinn. Our need to choose between good and evil presupposes that we are provided with the correct means to make the distinction. A merciful, kind and loving Creator would and has provided for all our needs in both the inner and outer worlds. As a source of external guidance we have prophets, messengers and revealed books. Internally we have the voice of the nafs (inner self) based in the heart.

> *"I encourage right and warn against evil and I am a guest in your heart. If you rebuke me when I speak, I shall depart. When invited in, I enter. Mine is the voice of Mercy and Truth, that echoes and reverberates in the whole of Creation and in the hearts of the Prophets and Messengers of Allah (as) and all believing souls."* [27]

Because the heart is like a systemic tuning fork, or the key to which all other parts are tuned, its condition will influence the condition of every other component of the being - thoughts, perceptions, feelings, desires, etc. as well as the physical organs and cells.

Healing, as we say in the wholistic field, occurs from the "top down and from the inside out". That is its direction. From the aspect of energy, it would move from the higher vibration to the lower. Physical matter registers on a relatively low vibrational level when compared with energy readings of invisible sources. Spiritual energy is conversely of an extremely high vibration as is love, an invisible, intangible emotion. Energy can be felt and each individual can feel and describe their energy level at any particular time. We can sense our own energy and that of others; we know when we are feeling "up" and when we are feeling "down". Each organ in the body has its own speed of vibration; its energy is calibrated at different levels. The heart must have the highest level so that it may regulate and influence the others. This is a principle of physics. Higher energies are capable of influencing objects or masses of lower energy but those of lower energy are not capable of influencing the higher energy sources except that they may drain that energy if it has no way of replenishing.

The heart's energy can be depleted. Ignoring its needs of spirituality and good association, refusing its direction and thus negating an essential part of its role in your life, will cause it to lose power and subsequently decline in health.

Chapter Five

Rhythms Of The Heart

وَلَقَدْ ءَاتَيْنَا دَاوُدَ مِنَّا فَضْلًا

يَـٰجِبَالُ أَوِّبِى مَعَهُۥ وَٱلطَّيْرَ ۖ وَأَلَنَّا لَهُ ٱلْحَدِيدَ ۝

"And certainly We bestowed on David a beautiful
gift from Us. 'Oh you mountains, sing back the
praises with him and you birds also.' And we
made the iron soft for him." (Quran Surah 34:10)

The words of Allah (swt) revealed to the Prophets and
Messengers (as) are melodic. Their very sound is striking
in pleasantness and their rhythm is magnetic. The messages of
the Creator are meant to reach the heart of man with their
soothing and compassionate verses and their severe warnings
and prohibitions. They will elicit deep-seated joy and profound
trembling in those with receptive hearts. All followers of the
Prophets are to take up their work and continue to relay the
message. In Quran we are instructed to read the verses with
measured rhythm[1] and the Prophet Muhammad (saw) has said that
Allah loves to hear the Quran recited in pleasant tones.[2]

93

Prophets spoke inspired words lyrical and beautiful, which softened the hearts, stimulated the minds, and drew the people back to their Lord. The Psalms of David (Zaboor), the Song of Solomon[3], and the rhythmic Ayat (verses) of the Generous Book[4] are known for their magnetic, calming, inspiring, and in the case of The Quran, healing effects. The Taurat (Torah) is chanted by specially trained individuals in Jewish religious ceremonies and even the translated Psalms to this day possess an inherent lyrical beauty. For example:

> *"Oh God, Though art my God. Early will I seek Thee, my soul thirsteth for Thee, my flesh longeth for Thee in a dry and thirsty land where no water is, to see Thy power and Thy glory so as I have seen Thee in the sanctuary. Because Thy loving kindness is better than life, my lips shall praise Thee."* [5]

The Prophet Dawood (as) was endowed with a beautiful voice, the like of which probably has never been heard again in the creation. I can say this because once Allah has given a Prophet a special, unique quality, that quality is never duplicated in another and also because the voice, like the fingerprint, is now known to be person specific.

94

The human voice is a remarkable instrument of change, transformation and healing. The vibrations of its sound can reach the heart and initiate changes, which reverberate throughout the entire system. Often, just the sound of a mother's voice is enough to change the mood of a distressed child. And remember the phenomenal softening of the hard heart of Hazrat Umar by the sound and message of the Quran being recited in his sister's home.[6] This, no doubt, was a combination of the divine content, the voice of a loved one and the ties between the hearts of a sister and brother. However, it was a historical event of such greatness that it inspired beautiful poetry, including that of Iqbal.

Human voices chanting and singing scripture, praise and prayer are soothing and uplifting to the spirit and heart as are the voices of all members of creation when understood and appreciated. As Allah (iwj) commanded the hills, mountains and birds to give praise, so have all things been given that command and taught the manner of their praise.

أَلَمْ تَرَ أَنَّ

اللَّهَ يُسَبِّحُ لَهُ مَنْ فِي السَّمَوَاتِ وَالْأَرْضِ وَالطَّيْرُ صَافَّاتٍ كُلٌّ قَدْ

عَلِمَ صَلَاتَهُ وَتَسْبِيحَهُ وَاللَّهُ عَلِيمٌ بِمَا يَفْعَلُونَ ﴿٤١﴾

"Don't you see that all beings in the heaven and earth glorify Allah, and the birds with their wings outstretched? Each one knows its own mode of prayer and praise and Allah knows all that they do." [7]

Allah's creation is a source of inspiration and instruction to us. Birds gave us the inspiration to seek a means of flight, the comfort of grass inspired carpet weaving and listening to nature inspired man to try to recreate the sounds which please the heart. Often the creation was even instructive in how to produce the necessary tools. There is a Native American saying that "The first flute was a gift of the woodpecker to the wind." [8] The original man-made music was the result of man attempting to reproduce the sounds of the environment. Thus, forest dwellers, responding to the myriad sounds of their surroundings, created instruments that produced polyphonic music. Mountain cultures yielded musical creations rich in bass tones and high frequency sounds, echoing the rhythms

96

of the peaks and valleys. Desert dwellers were the keepers of the undertone, having one common instrument – the omnipresent drum.[9] The undertone is the universal rhythm, which is the pulse of the world. It remains in simultaneous existence with the symphonic sounds of places and things – majestic mountains, rustling branches, humming fields, whispering breezes, etc. The basic rhythm remains constant; it is the heartbeat of the creation. The universe is inherently musical and rhythmic and all life moves and responds to its sounds. It is part of the innate knowledge of prayer, praise and worship. "The act of sincerely praising and glorifying Allah makes a person part of the universal refrain of praise echoed throughout the creation." [10] Experiencing this union is incredibly empowering and yet remarkably humbling.

Bio-Rhythm

As the fetus develops in its designated and protective enclosure, it is exposed to its own personal symphonic concert of wind, water, and rhythmic pulsing. The breathing of the mother, the rush and flow of the blood as it goes from and to the heart and the rhythms of her heartbeat becomes its daily concert along with external voices and sounds. As the fetus matures, it draws a sense of security from this dependable and constant blend of sounds. Once born, the child loves to rest on the mother's chest, there it can feel the rhythms of her breathing and the familiar heartbeat. Then it can relax and rest in a most contented state. The infant heart rate is quite rapid (100+ bpm), but the adult heart finds peace and contentment is the range of 60 – 70 bpm. Within this range the heart relaxes the body, calms the mind and maintains an inner environment where spontaneous healing can be generated.[11] It is also the range in which entrainment (synchronized working of the heart and brain) occurs.

The heart, as stated before, is attuned to a pulse generated by the Creator, and is responding to and communicating with all aspects of creation via energy pulsations and vibrations. We are all capable of hearing the voices of the creation but few do. Those who attune their faculties to the subtle voices and invent, create, write and compose as a result are labeled inspired. Their creations, whether scientific, literary or musical, can serve humanity and draw out a fondness for and attraction to themselves. Would you be willing to consider peanut butter? A creation of Dr. George Washington Carver, who said the plants spoke to him.[12] He produced hundreds of beneficial substances and items because he listened and responded to nature. Well, perhaps a Mozart concerto is more to your liking or the literature of William Shakespeare. The works of these two artists is now known to be particularly attractive because the rhythm of their works is the same as the rhythm of the peaceful heart. It is similarly so with some creations of great poets who wrote in iambic pentameter (i.e. John Keats, Robert Frost, A. Lord Tennyson and Walt Whitman). The alternating stress patterns of their work reflects the "lub-dub" pattern of the heartbeat.[13] We are naturally drawn to the rhythm but must take care to evaluate the content. Is the heart pleased or repulsed? Does it cause increased consciousness and virtuous thought? All things must be subjected to our inner system of furquan (Islamic criteria).

The heart needs and longs for rhythmic connections and reminders of its natural state. This century, Western medicine is reestablishing the link between sound and healing. In other cultures there has always been an understanding and practice of the use of sound for human healing. The centuries old art of Sufic chanting (dhikr) is used to attune body and spirit. Repetition of the "Sacred Formula" Laa ilaha illa Allah (There is no god except Allah), is said to be so effective because

> *"the long vowels of the words are primarily resonating in the heart, causing tremendous dissemination of divine attributes in a very short time. Moreover, the breath is compressed and condensed in a manner that generates a high degree of heat, which itself burns out many physical impurities."* [14]

Currently, the music of Mozart is being used in Europe and America to cure both psychological and physical illnesses.[15] They have found the violin concertos to be particularly effective.

Both of the above can be explained by the science of cymatics, the science of how sound and vibration interacts with matter. Vibrating sounds create movement in cells, tissues, and organs and actually begin to shape and sculpt matter in a variety of ways according to the tone, pitch, pulse and the areas being affected. The auditory nerve passes through the medulla and connects with all muscles of the body. The vagus nerve connects the ear with the larynx, heart, lungs, stomach, liver, bladder, kidneys, and small and large intestine.[16] This is why we can be so greatly affected by sound. Allah has said that the human being is fashioned from clay.[17] In general we are sculptable; capable of being reshaped, corrected or distorted. The heart is particularly responsive to sound; its rate increases or decreases according to the frequency and volume of the stimulus. Certain sounds calm and strengthen the heart, which then relays that message throughout the body. The lungs expand, the oxygen level increases, internal organs are energized and muscles relax. Other sounds will increase assonance and anxiety because they contradict the natural rhythm. The controversial but popular "heavy metal" music generally falls into this category.

In Florida, Dr. Ahmed El-Kadi has been studying the healing aspects of Quran from medical and scientific perspectives for over fifteen years. His research supports the beneficial effect of sound vibrations on the human body. Using three groups of listeners – Muslims who understood Arabic, Muslims who did not understand Arabic and non-Muslims- he played Quranic tapes. With testing of immune levels before and after the listening exercises, he found that every group experienced an improvement in the strength of the immune system.[18]

Universal Sound

"Tap into the heart's code and you will be able to sense the heartbeat of the forests, flowers and rocks." Paul Pearsall

We embody the rhythm of both the earth and the universe. The heart is the center of our own personal galaxy. We became acclimated to its rhythm as soon as the perceptive "ear" became functional. Our internal memories of those rhythms are what draws us to the mountains and the oceans where we sense the comfort of that previous environment. We seek to be re-tuned, find the serenity of reconnection with the rhythms of nature and reestablish our inner environment so that it is once again harmonious with the outer. When our internal rhythms are once again pulsating in synchrony, when our hearts are able to reestablish connections with the "outer," we feel ready again to interact with the rest of the world. This is the purpose of retreats – periods of withdrawal for personal realignment and recharging.

I recall a time of particular confusion and anxiety in my own life. I sought help by confiding in a friend, who had a degree in Shariah, Islamic Law, and who, I was sure, could give me sound advice. She did, but it was not from her formal education. She told me to go talk to nature. "Find a tree, a lake, anything and just talk out your problems." I went to the secluded public grounds of a monastery near my home and sat on a hill, under a tree and talked and cried. Certainly, I have no scientific explanation for the outcome, but I can tell you that when I left that place, I was not the same. Peace had reclaimed my anxious spirit and things no longer seemed so critical. So now, I too am one to "prescribe" time with nature. This somehow allows the subtle rhythmic exchange between our body and spirit and the forces of nature to re-sculpt us as they know we should be. It allows us to release the energy of negative emotions into the air and earth similar to the "grounding" that is said to occur during our salaat (formal prayers), when we are in the position of sujood (prostration).[19] We are earth and water and we are re-balanced and re-energized by our contact with these elements. We need to have this to some degree every day of our lives.

Chapter Six
The Ties That Bind

يَٰٓأَيُّهَا ٱلنَّاسُ ٱتَّقُواْ رَبَّكُمُ ٱلَّذِي خَلَقَكُم مِّن نَّفۡسٖ وَٰحِدَةٖ وَخَلَقَ مِنۡهَا زَوۡجَهَا وَبَثَّ مِنۡهُمَا رِجَالٗا كَثِيرٗا وَنِسَآءٗۚ وَٱتَّقُواْ ٱللَّهَ ٱلَّذِي تَسَآءَلُونَ بِهِۦ وَٱلۡأَرۡحَامَۚ إِنَّ ٱللَّهَ كَانَ عَلَيۡكُمۡ رَقِيبٗا ۝

"Oh you people, reverence you Guardian Lord,
Who created you from one soul and created from
her a mate and raised up from the two of them
numerous men and women." (Quran: Surah 4:1)

All of humanity has one common origin and regardless of how much we multiply or how far we spread out upon the earth, there remain divinely created, indestructible bonds between us. These bonds are in the oneness of our Lord and Creator, the common material from which we are created (earth and water), the intrinsic rhythm to which our hearts are set and the identical oath which we made to our Lord before entering this physical world.[1] These bonds may be strengthened or weakened by beliefs, actions, ignorance, awareness and so on, but never severed. In our humanness, we remain on equal footing and interdependent functioning with every other human being. The links between us are strengthened and increased in their level of quality and dignity as we join our hearts in faith, love, and kind service to one another.

وَٱعْتَصِمُوا بِحَبْلِ ٱللَّهِ جَمِيعًا وَلَا تَفَرَّقُوا

وَٱذْكُرُوا نِعْمَتَ ٱللَّهِ عَلَيْكُمْ إِذْ كُنتُمْ أَعْدَاءً فَأَلَّفَ بَيْنَ قُلُوبِكُمْ

فَأَصْبَحْتُم بِنِعْمَتِهِ إِخْوَانًا وَكُنتُمْ عَلَىٰ شَفَا حُفْرَةٍ مِّنَ ٱلنَّارِ

فَأَنقَذَكُم مِّنْهَا كَذَٰلِكَ يُبَيِّنُ ٱللَّهُ لَكُمْ ءَايَٰتِهِ لَعَلَّكُمْ تَهْتَدُونَ

﴿١٠٣﴾

"And hold fast to the rope of Allah and be not divided, and remember Allah's favor on you. For you were enemies and He joined your hearts (in love) so that you became, by His grace, brothers..." [2]

The joining of hearts is estimated to be one of the strongest, integrating, connective forces in the universe. Once this connection is made there remains an invisible stream of energy between the two entities, which endures as long as the physical life continues. [3] Because there is a frequency to every thought, feeling, sound, etc.,

106

it is very likely that the frequency of sincere iman bi Allah (belief in The One God) automatically causes a union between the Believers' hearts. This specific bonding has particular ways of being strengthened.

Salaat (obligatory prayers) Performed in Congregation

Every reflective, knowledge-seeking Believer is convinced of the multiple benefits of the group prayer. It's social benefit is visually obvious as it causes people to come together and unite behind one leader enforcing a structure to the community, while individuals engage in unified worship. The Prophet (saw) said that the prayer of the group is 27 times more beneficial than the prayer said alone.[4] As Muslims we do not dispute the truth of the Prophet's words and understand that we may never comprehend the extent of these benefits. However, like Prophet Ibraheem (as) as he asked the Lord to show him how he gave life after death,[5] we may be curious.

In unrelated research there is confirmation of the Prophet's statement and an easy example for our understanding. In the field of Sociology, one researcher's study of the family led him to say, "Observable, repetitive, positive behaviors, which recur with predictable regularity in day to day life are conducive to health - emotional and physical." [6] When the same behavior is repeated in the same way, by the same people there is an energy that bonds the participants and its composite is extremely powerful. This energy takes on a character similar to that of a laser, which has an unusual power because its light waves are in complete synchronicity. Faith groups and families are at their highest energetic point when they come together in prayer and worship of the Creator. In this effort the heart dominates because it is the center of communion and conversation with the Lord. When the hearts' energies join, a great power arises from which each individual will benefit. The Christian adage "The family that prays together, stays together" is a truth that can be extended to the community.

The benefit of repetitive acts is also applicable to joining the Friday prayers (a weekly gathering), participating in the annual fast of Ramadan, etc. Also, there is a particular power derived from du'ah made with the hands open and raised. The palms of the hands have great capacity for conduction and transmission of energy. When the palms are up, they serve as natural electrodes attracting the divine, universal answers to our pleas and requests. This energy is immediately transmitted to the heart, which finds a wonderful satisfaction and peace from it. Anyone who has participated in group du'ah can bear witness to this fact. In the past I have been able to feel that power just by listening to a recording of the du'ah of Lailah-tul-Qadr[7] made at the Haram in Makkah. Those who were present must have been quivering with the energy of the dhikr (remembrance of Allah) and afterwards felt the tranquil heart of a blessed calm.[8] Here in the United States, I spoke with a number of people who had that experience when a du'ah was made after Salaat at an ISNA Convention held at McCormick Place in Chicago (September 1999). The Imam conducted a chanted du'ah in English, which was both beautiful and powerful. There was an estimated participation of several thousand drawing universal energies, which are at the service of the servants of Allah.

Wholistic healers are frequently trained in the use of their hands as transmitters of energy (as well as in other therapeutic techniques). Our understanding in terms of this energy transfer healing is that we are not using our own energy but a healing power conducted through us from the universe. We conduct energy from the earth and the heavens and allow it to pass through our electrical system and pour forth through our hands. Everyone is conducting energy all the time, but healers have a greater capacity to attract specific energies at will (with Allah's permission) and are allowed to use these forces for the healing of others. The submission and humility of our hearts has a great deal to do with our capability and effectiveness. My personal course in this technique was titled "Healing Rays of Light" but I have always called it "Laser Healing" because some recipients have expressed that it feels like a beam of warm light passing through their body.

This power to attract and disperse energy is present in the group. Together the individuals send forth from their hearts an energy that comes as if from one great heart, united and strong. That force can then cut through and destroy diseases of the community and even affect the healing of the world. Our Merciful Guardian has said,:

وَإِذَا سَأَلَكَ

عِبَادِى عَنِّى فَإِنِّى قَرِيبٌ أُجِيبُ دَعْوَةَ ٱلدَّاعِ إِذَا دَعَانِّ

فَلْيَسْتَجِيبُواْ لِى وَلْيُؤْمِنُواْ بِى لَعَلَّهُمْ يَرْشُدُونَ ﴿١٨٦﴾

"And when my servant asks you about me, I am indeed near. I answer the call of every supplicant when he calls to Me. Then let them answer Me and believe in Me that they may be rightly guided." [9]

The lone worshipper is vulnerable like the stray sheep attacked by the wolf. However, two or more draw a protective covering from the unseen world and lend strength to each other. We must never underestimate the power of joint worship. The Prophet (saw) has said that 12,000 Muslims united (as one heart) can not be defeated.[10] We have gatherings greater than this in some cities here in the

United States at least twice a year but where is our effect? Our hearts have not yet reached the necessary level. The heart must first purify and right the individual in which it resides, then it will join with other purified and righteous hearts. When this happens, there is nothing in this universe that can have a sufficient opposing force.

Greetings and Kindness

The Prophet Muhammad (saw) said, **"Shall I tell you of a thing, when you do it will increase love between you? Spread the 'Salaam' (greeting of peace) between each other."** [11] Muhammad (saw) was sent as a mercy to the worlds (rahmatun lil 'alameen). Before and after his mission of prophethood was revealed to him, he was known as a kind-hearted individual. He looked after the orphans, visited the sick, and fed the needy; whether they were from his own tribe or complete strangers. This earned him respect in the eyes of friends and enemies alike. Kindness exchanged between people will cause their hearts to soften and love will grow between them, sometimes in spite of their own stubbornness. It is a universal law, an automatic

function inherent in this universe. Allah ta'alaa says,

وَمَنْ أَحْسَنُ قَوْلًا مِّمَّن دَعَآ إِلَى ٱللَّهِ وَعَمِلَ صَلِحًا وَقَالَ

إِنَّنِى مِنَ ٱلْمُسْلِمِينَ ۝ وَلَا تَسْتَوِى ٱلْحَسَنَةُ وَلَا ٱلسَّيِّئَةُ

ٱدْفَعْ بِٱلَّتِى هِىَ أَحْسَنُ فَإِذَا ٱلَّذِى بَيْنَكَ وَبَيْنَهُ عَدَاوَةٌ كَأَنَّهُۥ

وَلِىٌّ حَمِيمٌ ۝

"Who is better in speech than one who calls to
Allah, works righteousness and says 'I am of those
who submit their wills (are Muslim)'. Nor can
goodness and evil be equal. Repel evil with good.
Then one between you and him was hatred will
become as a caring friend." [12]

We should all give some attention to the product of our tongues

and remind ourselves of the purpose for which the tongue was

created. Imam Al-Ghazali believed and wrote in his great work,

Ihyaa Uloom Ud Deen, that all units and organs (of the body)

receiving information are servants and soldiers of the heart. [13] The

tongue is used both for taste and for speech. In one capacity it

brings in information of pleasure, delight or disgust and in the

other, it sends out information. It is a servant without doubt

and it becomes our choice as to who or what will be its master.

We are informed by the Hadith that the greeting of Salaam is one of divine origin, used by angels, prophets, and the inhabitants of Paradise.[14] We are instructed to use it and respond to it. Then as another sign of its importance, the Prophet (saw) has given detailed instruction as to the etiquette of it:

> *"The young should greet the old, the passer by should greet the sitting one and the small group of persons should greet the larger group of persons."* [15]

So, why is it that some Muslims withhold this right from their sister or brother and cut off their own blessings by refraining from this simple act? Cultural impositions that have subdued this aspect of the Islamic character and a desire to hide their Islamic identity in the non-Islamic countries and societies are several possible answers. The hearts are paying a high price for such foolishness. Why not test the Prophet's words, which opened this sub-section, and see what happens just as a result of making this beautiful greeting a part of your habit and that of your children? At the very least we must respond to a greeting, for in doing so is obedience to Allah (iwj) and recognition of Allah as our Rabb (Guardian Lord). We accept a great depth of wisdom and benefit in these words:

114

وَإِذَا حُيِّيتُم بِتَحِيَّةٍ فَحَيُّواْ
بِأَحْسَنَ مِنْهَآ أَوْ رُدُّوهَآ إِنَّ ٱللَّهَ كَانَ عَلَىٰ كُلِّ شَىْءٍ حَسِيبًا ﴿٨٦﴾

"When you are greeted with a greeting, then return it with one that is better than it or (at least) return it equally. Surely, Allah is taking account of all things." [16]

As Muslims, we have the best of all possible greetings, whose minimum is salaam or peace and security, and the betterment of it is rahmah and barakah (mercy and blessings) of Allah.

To adequately address the topic of kindness would involve extensive writing. Kindness is a virtue of great magnitude and yet can be expressed in simple acts such as meeting others with a smile, visiting the sick or acting with justice and fairness. In these and all other acts of kindness done for the sake of Allah are blessings for the one offering and the one receiving. None of us is so poor that we have nothing to offer, unless our hearts are harder than the concrete we walk on.

Enjoining Right and Forbidding Wrong

The heart is the seat of intuitive knowledge and receiver of Divine instruction. It is from where comes our direction of right and wrong and the source of our furqaan (discerning ability). It is our faith and use of this discernment that will qualify us for the noble position of "the best people brought forth from humanity." [17]

Coming together acting as one unified body to achieve something of good cements the hearts. Whoever has worked with others in such a way will know what was experienced within themselves and between the members of their group. One derives a powerful energizing feeling from being in a group of people or family with whom there is spiritual, emotional, and physical comfort and shared goals. Allah strengthens the efforts of those who believe and do right and weakens the effects of the wrongdoers. There are times when this may not seem to be the case but we are told not to "lose heart nor fall into despair" [18] for Allah's promise is true. Our actions may be as simple as boycotting a local business that has treated an employee with injustice or as great as supporting the Jihad for Islamic independence and human rights in places like Chechnya, Cashmere, Palestine, Bosnia, etc. There may be an immediate result or the effort may not be rewarded for twenty years but the words of Allah remain true. If we remain dedicated to righteousness, our hearts will remain tied and our strength will not decrease.

Friendship: Chosen Companions

The integrative heart is always seeking connection with others and not just any connection but lasting, beneficial ones. Prolonged isolation and a lack of physical association will deprive the heart of energetic replenishment. Short term and broken relationships drain the heart's energy and leave it in a sad and lonely state. Companionship, however, will only be of benefit when we select those of honorable character, those who are also Believers. Actually, the healthy heart will allow no other connection; it will be repulsed by and seek to distance itself from disbelievers and those of low morals. In some way our spiritual selves resonate with others of like spirit and find peace and joy in their presence. These positive interactions attract energies and healing forces capable of neutralizing many harmful influences of the physical world, including depression and disease. If we learn to pay attention to our own feelings, we will notice that we feel energized, upbeat and relaxed in the presence of some and confused, nervous and heavy with others. The saying, "a man is judged by the company he keeps," is ancient wisdom true in this life as well as being indicative of our condition in the next. For, we are bound to those with whom we choose to associate. Friendship can serve us well or be a source of our destruction. When Allah (swt) says in the Quran,

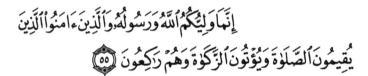

"With certainty, your friends are Allah, and His Messenger and those who believe, the ones who establish their salaat and give zakaat and they bow down (in humble worship)." [19]

then we know that it is these, and these only, who will bring strength and health to our hearts. Our spiritual challenge is to interact consciously with others using the intellect of the heart. In this way we will form unions with those who support our righteousness, health and positive development and release or sever relationships that handicap our growth, progress and healing processes.

Marriage

Next to the bond between parent and child, the bond between the hearts of a husband and wife are the strongest in love and devotion. The basis of marriage lies in the nurturing, nourishing, soothing qualities of "mawadatan wa rahmah" (love and mercy), which Allah Himself places between these hearts.[20] Within and by enactment of the blessedness of this union, the hearts and bodies are energized and the spirit is encouraged. Allah, the Source of all Love, has ordained marriage and put Divine blessing in it and, yet, we find so many distressed hearts lingering in decayed and decaying relationships devoid of love. Allah speaks in Quran of desiring to complete His grace to us.[21] The grace and blessing of marriage is joy, happiness, peace, comfort, fulfillment of desires, sharing, healing, protection, and encouragement to do more of good, give more in service to our Lord and to love more.

Marriage is a re-creation of the relationship established between the first human beings, Adam and Hawwa (Eve). Allah (swt) intended for them to support each other on all levels of their existence — physical, mental, and spiritual. Marriage was originated by Allah, ordained by Allah and is blessed by Allah in its joys and trials. However, most of what occurs in a marriage is what is brought into it by the two individuals.

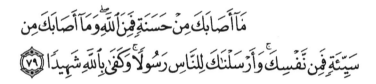

"Whatever happens to you of good is from Allah.
But whatever evil happens is from your own soul" [22]

The best outcome of any endeavor is heavily influenced by the character and intentions of those involved. The best way to avoid difficulties and unpleasant consequences of our actions and choices is to enter into them with wisdom, purity of heart and pure intentions. In marriage, it is important to become familiar with the advice and instructions that Allah (swt) and His Prophet (saw) have given related to the selection of a spouse. Then the choice should be made based on Divine criteria and one's specific needs. We must seek to find the zawj (complementary half) that Allah (iwj) has placed for us in the creation. When we seek Allah's help with the du'ah of Istikhara [23], we must then become willing recipients of the guidance. "Any choice made from faith has the full power of heaven behind it." [24] Iman (faith) resides in the heart. Allah's guidance to our souls is transmitted through the heart. We must carefully examine ourselves to see what is the dominant desire motivating our choice, for often it is not the desires of the heart but those of the body or the materially dominated brain. Our desires, biases, even our preferences must be temporarily set aside to allow and assure Divine intervention and guidance. Allah knows and we do not know, but we can be taught, if we allow ourselves to receive Divine education. Quieting the self and its barrage of chatter will allow the Divine voice to be heard more clearly. "Slow down, sit down, quiet down. There is nothing so like God as stillness." [25]

I have personally learned what I think is good advice to pass on. When your own voices and perceptions, corrupted by the distortions and perversions of a lifetime, seek to take authority in defining reality and forming a basis for decisions, abandon them. Find pure truths on which to focus, repeat those truths to yourself and call on Al-Haqq, the True Reality. The Shahadah, Laa ilaha illa Allah, is a pure truth; every word and ayat of the Quran is a pure truth; universal, unchanging laws are pure truth; the fact that Allah desires our right guidance is pure truth. The more we focus on truth, the less room there will be for a lie to take hold in our heart and mind. The energy of truth is such that it creates an environment where lies cannot exist. As Allah tell us in Quran, truth will destroy falsehood. [26]

We are in need of truth at all times but particularly in the selection of a mate for life. We need to know the truth of the heart to which we intend to join our own treasured heart and this truth can come with a concentrated quietness.

> *"When we are still enough to establish the cardio-coherence that makes us peaceful enough to love and be loved and allow ourselves to suspend the brain's defensive vigilance and arrogant prejudices, then we can become more aware of what our heart is trying to tell us about another heart and compassionate enough to be receptive to the subtle energy coming from that heart."* [27]

A true "heart to heart" conversation will yield all the truth we need. However, we must realize that even with our best efforts and adherence to the commands of Allah (swt) and the advice of the Prophet (saw), we will evolve and change and so will our spouses. Two righteous people can become uncomfortable with each other and their hearts will be in states of anxiety. When all reasonable efforts to heal a relationship are exhausted and two people find that peace, joy, and love are no longer present in their marriage, then it is time to separate with kindness. Involving oneself in avoidable misery and suffering does not bring personal benefit, nor does it serve the world. It is our duty to have a healthy heart that gives

123

and receives love and mercy. Remember that Allah wants nothing less than our complete happiness, harmony, peace and wholeness. Learn to recognize love by experiencing Allah's love. It is inextricably woven into all of the creation and can be felt in the warmth of the sun, the gentleness of the breeze the shade of a tree, the song of the birds, the service of an animal and the sweetness of a fruit. It also flows through others that have been placed in your life, even for brief moments, who have loving and giving hearts. Love is greatly misunderstood and its name is frequently attached to desires and motives that are not even related to love. Know that love is gentle, supportive, protective, peaceful, kind, generous, nurturing, healing, and comfortable. It brings a sense of peace and joy into our lives. It is encouraging, energizing and accepting of our shortcomings. Love is also abundant and therefore should not be in short supply or meted out in small increments. When you find yourself experiencing the opposite of these beautiful and uplifting energies, then you need to carefully examine the situation and the person, and reconsider. Most importantly, you must realize that loving yourself as a creation and servant of Allah is a prerequisite for being able to recognize the same coming from the outside.

Comments

In choosing the above sub-topics describing actions that will strengthen the heart, I in no way mean to indicate that I have completed or exhausted the possibilities. There are many things, both large and small, that could be included in this section including other forms of dhikr (remembrance), increasing the taqwa (consciousness), etc. I have only given a few examples, which I felt should be prominent in the lives of every Believer. Another book could be written on this topic alone. Suffice it to say that heart tonics and medications could be reduced by following another method of achieving a strong, healthy heart.

Chapter Seven

The Heart Secured and Peaceful

يَـٰٓأَيَّتُهَا ٱلنَّفۡسُ ٱلۡمُطۡمَئِنَّةُ ۝ ٱرۡجِعِىٓ
إِلَىٰ رَبِّكِ رَاضِيَةً مَّرۡضِيَّةً ۝ فَٱدۡخُلِى فِى عِبَـٰدِى ۝ وَٱدۡخُلِى جَنَّتِى ۝

"Oh you soul in complete serenity, return to your Lord pleased and pleasing. Then enter amongst My servants and enter My garden"
(Quran; 89: 27 - 30)

The soul described above is the one that has achieved the ultimate goal of life. It has successfully prompted the heart and the heart in willing cooperation has been able to guide the human body in which it resided. While the heart always has its reasoning ability which reason (brain) may not know, the self conscious must learn to accept that the heart has a purpose and

strives to reach a specific goal. Every community has its Imam
(leader) and the community of self has the heart. As the Prophet
(saw) informed us regarding the heart, "If it is right, it will right the
entire body." [1] The heart allowed to respond to Divine guidance
and universal direction (fitrah) will maintain a state of health and
harmony of the body and spirit. The heart prompts and guides our
physical awareness and actions as the soul moves through its stages
of consciousness on its spiritual goal of becoming the director and
guide of our physical life. Allah (swt) has said that we will definitely
move through stages.

فَلَآ أُقْسِمُ بِالشَّفَقِ ۝ وَالَّيْلِ وَمَا وَسَقَ ۝ وَالْقَمَرِ إِذَا اتَّسَقَ ۝ لَتَرْكَبُنَّ طَبَقًا عَن طَبَقٍ ۝ فَمَا لَهُمْ لَا يُؤْمِنُونَ ۝

*"So I swear by the glow of sunset, and by the night
and what it gathers, and by the moon in its
fullness. You shall certainly travel from stage to
stage."* [2]

The heart works to assist the soul so that it can return to its Lord in
a pleasing state.

Path to Peace

As human beings endowed with freedom of choice, we have a heavy responsibility. We are expected to exert ourselves and discipline our internal state, which will then govern our words and actions. Much of what will happen in our lives will depend upon this internal state and the ultimate outcome of our lives is absolutely dependent on it. Thus, it can be said that we are largely responsible for our own destiny. [3] We are each individually responsible for our final record and balance and this responsibility begins as soon as our conscious self understands right from wrong. The core of this internal development is named in the Quran as "nafsul lawammah" (self accusing soul - pushing towards right). [4] It is described as a soul searching for truth and clarity, sometimes confused and vacillating between right and wrong, depending on what force is dominant in the individual. [5] Allah begins to hold us accountable because we have had some time to develop a discerning ability and are physically moving from the stage of childhood to the beginnings of adulthood. At this point we move from external responsibility (parents, family, etc.) for our actions to personal responsibility for all actions, thoughts, and feelings. Even with bad parenting and lack of proper moral education, inner wisdom will guide one to righteous thought through discomfort, curiosity, and observance. This inner voice, coming through the heart, will strive hard to correct all wrong programming and false ideas. It will prompt correct choices and push one to seek new information and circumstances. It remains aware of the fact that when we return to our Lord we will not be able to put blame on any one or even the society in which we lived. Each soul will bear its own burden. [6] We may be challenged by our birth circumstances, etc. but not crippled.

The Battle of Good and Evil

While this consciousness and push for pure goodness is advancing, the opposite and opposing force will inevitably arise. That is the negative force of the "nafsul ammarah" (soul prone to evil)[7], prompted by suggestions and deception of Shaitan, it is attracted to indulgence of base desires, falsehoods and self-glorification. The self must be subjected by recognition of Divine authority and by devotion to its Creator. The heart and soul must be allowed intimate interaction by the conscious choice of each individual. This desire for goodness in the physical world is the exclusive domain of the heart. It is the origin of good intentions, which are the root of every good action and the basis on which Allah will judge our deeds. [8] "Learn about intentions, for their importance is greater than the importance of the action itself." [9] The purest of intentions is that all of what is done is only for the pleasure of The Lord and not for any other reason. The righteous heart is ale to summon such intentions most of the time and, because of that, small acts become great. Of course, conversely, some acts that appear to be of great magnitude will be rendered insignificant because of the desire for personal gain, public recognition or even baser desires.

The battle of right vs. wrong, truth vs. falsehood, and life vs. death will continue for the balance of our lives and indeed for the duration of all human existence. It is simply a continuation of the struggle between man and Satan that originated in the Garden.

Purifiers of the Heart

Truth is undoubtedly one of the great purifiers. It encompasses every reality and excludes all delusion, confusion and falsehood. Truth and light are synonymous and bring joy to the heart. Lies in any form are immediately recognized by our spiritual and biological systems and rejection responses are initiated. We are created in truth and function optimally on truth alone. This has great and far reaching significance on the heart and health of the human being. Think for a moment on the immune system and how it rejects and seeks to destroy any intruder or false resident in the body. This includes the substances of blood transfusions and transplanted organs. See how the self tries be free of the burden of psychological oppression imposed by lies (i.e. "You are not worthy."; "You are not loved.", etc.). This goes on and on even to encompass entire social systems and is too extensive to address here. However, it is important to note that even the seeking of truth increases the purity and, therefore, the health of the heart. Prophet Abraham (as) was born into a corrupted religious society. His own father created idols used for community worship but

Allah describes Ibraheem (as) in the midst of this mess as one with "qalbun saleem" (a pure heart).

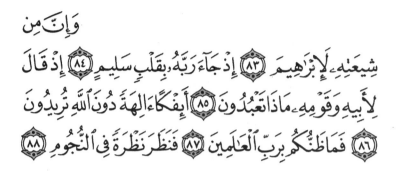

"And, verily, among those who followed his (Nuh's/Noah's) way was Ibraheem, when he came to his Lord with a pure heart, when he said to his father and to his people, "What is it that you worship? Is it a falsehood that you desire?" [10]

He evaluated the situation in his community, recognized it as false and sought after the truth. This process purified his heart and prepared it to accept pure truth. This process will do the same for any of us and, as a result, will strengthen our biological heart. This is because the spiritual energy and benefits cannot be separated from our biological self. The spiritual aspect of our existence is the energetic basis of our lives. It is the energy which initially animates all biological matter and continues to sustain that life. We exist simultaneously as matter and spirit in continual integrated interaction. When the higher self receives a benefit, that energy flows downward into the physical realm. The heart infused with spiritual energy will become closer to the desired state of "qalbun saleemun" (a heart pure and pleasing).

Supporting the Evolution

There is assistance available in the process. Love of the goodness of the Creator, love of all good things and the pleasure in pleasing our Lord creates tremendous joy in the heart. Sincere love of good brings the heart and soul into perfect synchronization. Increase of knowledge and development of our intellect and perception facilitate this ability to love; and dedication to the role of servant causes us to base our lives in truth. Attempting to give another purpose to our life will take its toll on our physical body and conscious mind. Some of the most serious cases I have worked with and continue to encounter are those of individuals who have allowed another "lord" in their lives and have become servants to someone or something other than Allah (The One God).

They usually are resigned to a life lacking in true joy and happiness. There is even a lack of awareness of what is the heart's desire.

Servitude to the Creator creates a happy humility that brings deep inner pleasure and ease in performing worldly duties. It is a wonderful facilitator to the difficult journey of life.

Stillness and Contemplation

We frequently use the term brilliant in praise of one's demonstration of and application of learned knowledge. Quieting the mind and stilling the heart agitators is described by Dr. Paul Pearsall as "a brilliant silence." [11] The heart in comfort and quiet can begin a process of purification and renewal. The physical body can lend assistance to this process by sitting or standing upright with the head, neck and spine in alignment. This posture increases the ability to listen and stimulates full consciousness. "The entire body becomes a receptive antenna" [12] unified to serve the purpose of the heart. What we need to learn is what brings comfort to the heart and seek these things in the "brilliant silence." Allah ('iwj) is specific with this information and its benefits.

وَيَقُولُ

ٱلَّذِينَ كَفَرُواْ لَوْلَآ أُنزِلَ عَلَيْهِ ءَايَةٌ مِّن رَّبِّهِۦ قُلْ إِنَّ ٱللَّهَ يُضِلُّ مَن يَشَآءُ وَيَهْدِىٓ إِلَيْهِ مَنْ أَنَابَ ﴿٢٧﴾ ٱلَّذِينَ ءَامَنُواْ وَتَطْمَئِنُّ قُلُوبُهُم بِذِكْرِ ٱللَّهِ أَلَا بِذِكْرِ ٱللَّهِ تَطْمَئِنُّ ٱلْقُلُوبُ ﴿٢٨﴾

> *"Truly He allows to go astray whom He wills and guides to Himself who turns to him in repentance; those who believe and whose hearts find satisfaction and comfort in the remembrance of Allah. And surely in the remembrance of Allah do hearts find comfort and satisfaction."* [13]

With similar meaning the Old Testament record of a Psalm of David reads,

> *"Delight in the Lord and he will give you the heart's desire."* [14]

Peacefulness of the heart is the greatest treasure we can ever acquire. Whether we have been previously aware of it or not, let us now acknowledge that the heart's desire is to serve the soul and purify the body so that both may return to their Lord in a pleasing manner. We can use the words of our Father in faith, Ibraheem (Abraham) and pray as he prayed,

رَبِّ هَبْ لِى حُكْمًا وَأَلْحِقْنِى بِالصَّلِحِينَ ۝ وَاجْعَل لِّى لِسَانَ صِدْقٍ فِى ٱلْءَاخِرِينَ ۝ وَاجْعَلْنِى مِن وَرَثَةِ جَنَّةِ ٱلنَّعِيمِ ۝ وَاغْفِرْ لِأَبِى إِنَّهُ كَانَ مِنَ ٱلضَّآلِّينَ ۝ وَلَا تُخْزِنِى يَوْمَ يُبْعَثُونَ ۝ يَوْمَ لَا يَنفَعُ مَالٌ وَلَا بَنُونَ ۝ إِلَّا مَنْ أَتَى ٱللَّهَ بِقَلْبٍ سَلِيمٍ ۝

"My Lord, bestow wisdom on me and join me with the righteous and grant me honorable mention in generations to come. And make me one of the inheritors of the Paradise of Delight. And, forgive my father, surely he is of the misguided. And do not disgrace me on the day of resurrection, the day when neither wealth nor children will be of any benefit. But only he (will succeed) who brings to Allah a secured and peaceful heart." (15)

This is a prayer that is beneficial to be repeated throughout one's life. It is one that, if answered, guarantees true success. A manifestation of Allah's love and mercy in this world and perfect joy in the next. What more can a sincere heart desire?

End Notes
Chapter One

1. In the early stages of the fetal development of the heart, a mass of cells form tubes, and constricts until the five regions of the heart become distinct. <u>Human Anatomy</u>; 2nd Edition; Kent M. Van de Graff; Wm. C.. Brown Publishers; 1984

2. Ibid.;

3. <u>Scientific American</u>; August 1994; p. 46

4. J. Lacey and B. Lacey; <u>Conversations Between the Heart and Brain</u>; Bulletin of the National Institute of Mental Health; Rockville, MD; March 1987

5. Linda G. Russek and Gary E. Schwartz; <u>Energy Cardiology: A Dynamic Energy Systems Approach</u>...; Advances Vol. 12:1996; pp. 4–24

6. Doc Lew Childre; <u>Freeze Frame</u>;

7. The sinoatrial node located at the top of the right atrium; the center and source of its neural energy

8. Cheng Xennong, Chief Editor; <u>Chinese Acupuncture and Moxibustion</u>; Foreign Language Press; Beijing, China; 1987; pp. 26-27, 37 or For a   layman's understanding of Oriental Medicine, I recommend <u>The Web That Has No Weaver</u>

9.   Doc Lew Childre; <u>Freeze Frame</u>; IHM; 1994;

10. Quran; Surah An-Najm (#53, The Star):39

11. As quoted on NBC World News with Peter Jennings; March 3,
     1999

End Notes
Chapter Two

1. Quran; Surah Baqarah (#2, The Cow): Ayah 31

2. Deepak Chopra; The Seven Spiritual Laws of Success; Amber Allen Publishing; 1994 p. 44

3. Ibid. p. 43

4. Iyanla Van Zandt, author of One Day My Soul Just Opened Up and other books.

5. Quran; Surah Nahl (#16, The Bee): Ayah 78

6. Yusuf Ali; Footnote to Quranic Verse; Chapter 46: Verse 26

7. Translated portion of Quran; Verse 46 of Surah 22

8. Quran; Surah Hijr (#15, The Rocky Tracts): Ayah 97 and Surah An-Naas (#114 Mankind): Ayah 5

9. Quran; Surah Al-Mulk (#67, The Kingdom):23

10. Ibid.; Surah Inshirah (#94 Expansion): Ayah 1

11. Ibid.; Surah Al-Hajj (#20 The Pilgrimage): Ayah 46

12. Paul Pearsall, MD; The Heart's Code; Broadway Books; 1998; p.

13. Quran; Surah An-Nur (#24 The Light): Ayah 35

14. Ibid.; Surah Al-Baqarah (#2 The Cow): Ayat 6 – 7

15. Ibid.; Surah Al-Baqarah (#2 The Cow): Ayat 97

16. Ibid.; Surah Al-Shu'araa (#26 The Poets):192-194

17. Abdullah Yusuf Ali; Translation and Commentary of Quran; Note #3225 to   Ayah 194

18. Paul Pearsall, MD; The Heart's Code; Broadway Books;1996

19. Quran; Surah Ibraheem (#14 Abraham);Ayah 7

20. Ibid.; Surah Al-Mu'min (#40 The Faithful One): Ayah 35

21. Ibid.; Surah Jaathiyah (#45 The Bending of the Knee): Ayah 23

22. Both Deepak Chopra and Barbara Ann Brennan use their knowledge and understanding of physics to help explain the physical condition in their writings.

23. Quran; Surah An-Nahl (#16 The Bee): Ayah 108

End Notes
Chapter Three

1. Paul Pearsall; <u>The Heart's Code</u>; Broadway Books; 1998; p.36

2. Andrew Weil; <u>Spontaneous Healing</u>; Alfred A. Knopf; 1995; pp. 208-209

3. Quran; Surah Al-Fath (#48 The Victory):Ayah 29

4. Ibid.; Surah Taubah(#9 Repentance):Ayah 71

5. Muhammad Haykal; <u>The Life of Muhammad</u>; N.A. Trust Publications; 1978; pp 227-228

6. Bear Heart; <u>The Wind Is My Mother</u>; Clarkson Potter; 1996; pp. 134-135

7. Irish Medical Journal; Vol. #77; 1984; pp. 316-318

8. Paul Pearsall; <u>The Heart's Code</u>; Broadway Books; 1998; p. 16

9. Quran; Surah Rum (#30 Rome):Ayah 41

10. Fazlur Rahman; <u>Health and Medicine in the Islamic Tradition</u>; Crossroad; 1989

11. Hadith of Prophet Muhammad; Sahih of Al-Bukharee; Vol. I: Book of Belief: #1

12. Quran; Surah Bani Israil (#17 The Tribe of Israel:Ayah 44

13. Hadith of Prophet Muhammad; *(...Prayer is light)*

14. Sarah Ban Breathnach; Simple Abundance; Warner Books; 1995; February 4

15. Barbara Ann Brennan; Hands of Light; Bannam; 1987; p. 43

16. Carl Jung

17. Quran; Surah Al-Kahf (#18 The Cave):Ayah 28

End Notes
Chapter Four

1. Chinese Acupuncture and Moxibustion; Chief Editor Cheng Xinong; Foreign Language Press; Beijing, China; 1996; pp 18 - 21

2. Deepak Chopra; <u>Seven Spiritual Laws of Success</u>; 1994; p. 107

3. Doc Lew Childre; <u>Freeze Frame</u>; Institute of Heart Math; 1994; p. 42

4. An-<u>Nawawi's Forty Hadith</u>; An Anthology; No. 16

5. Paul Pearsall; <u>The Heart's Code</u>; Broadway Books; 1998

6. Sahih Muslim; Anthology of Hadith; Vol.

7. For more information read <u>The Heart's Code</u> and <u>Does Changing the Heart Mean Changing the Personality</u>

8. Translated from El Coran; Venezuela;

9. Don Campbell; <u>The Mozart Effect</u>; Avon Books; 1997; p. 26

10. Sahih Al-Bukhari:Vol. 7: 309

11. Muhammed Al Ghazali; Muslim Character; IFSO;p. 29

12. Abdul Fattah R. Hamid; Self Knowledge and Spiritual Yearning; ATP; p. 74

13. Quran: Surah Al-Zukhruf (#43 The Gold Ornaments): 36-37

14. Paul Pearsall; The Heart's Code; Broadway Books; 1998

15. For Laghwun (vain talk) see Quran Surah Al-Mu'minoon (#23 The Believers) 1-3

16. Quran; Surah Al-Waqi'ah (#56 The Inevitable Event):25-26

17. Tirmidhi; Hadith No. 1244

18. Quran; Surah An-Nur (#24 The Light):30 - 31

19. Ibid.; Surah Al-Taubah (#9 Repentance):23

20. Ibid.; Surah Al-Ma'idah (#5 The Tablespread):57

21. Ibid.; Surah Al-Ra'ad (#13 The Thunder):28

22. Ibid.; Surah Al-Baqarah (#2 The Cow):260

23. Ibid.; Surah Al-Zariaat (#51 The Winds That Scatter):56

24. Ibid.; Surah Al-Baqarah (#2 The Cow):30

25. Ibid.; Surah Al-Hajj (#22 The Pilgrimage):78

26. Purification of the Soul; Compilation of Works of Ibn Rajab Al-Hanbali, Ibn AlQayyim Al-Jawziyyah and Abu Hamid AlGhazali; Collected by Ahmed Farid; Al-Firdaus Ltd.; London; 1993

27. Abdul Fattah R. Hamid; Self Knowledge and Spiritual Yearning; ATP; p. 23

147

End Notes

Chapter Five

1. Quran: Surah Al-Muzzammil (#73 – The One Folded in Garments):Ayah 4

2. Sahih Bukharee; Volume 6; p. 500

3. Book of the Old Testament

4. Another name for the Quran

5. Old Testament; Psalm #63; A Thirst For God

6. Muhammad Haykal; The Life of Muhammad; N.A. Trust Publications; 1978; pp 103-104

7. Quran; Surah An-Nur (#24 The Light):Ayah 41

8. Tribal Winds: Music from Native American Flutes; CD – Producer David Swenson; 1995

9. Campbell, Don; The Mozart Effect; Avon Books; 1997; p.40

10. Hamid, Abdul-Fattah; Self Knowledge and Spiritual Yearning; American Trust Publications; p. 14

11. As healing agents we learned that the body heals best when it is relaxed. I personally begin each session with a sequence of accupressure on the head and shoulders de signed to ease tension and prepare the body for a health stimulating session.

12. Clark, Glenn; The Man Who Talked With The Flowers: The Life Story of George Washington Carver; Macalester Park Publishing; 1994

13. Campbell, Don; The Mozart Effect; pp. 67-68

14. Chisti, Hakim Moinuddin; The Book of Sufi Healing; Inner Traditions Intern'l; 1985; pp. 145-146

15. Campbell, Don; The Mozart Effect; pp. 19-20, 32, etc. References are throughout the book.

16. Van der Graff, Ken; Human Anatomy; pp.372-373

17. Quran; Surah Al-Hijr (#15 The Rocky Tract):Ayah 26

18. Ahmed El-Qadi; Quran and Wellness; Presented to ISNA Convention;1985

19. Ahmed Sakr; Sujood; Foundation of Islamic Knowledge; 1997;p. 58

End Notes
Chapter Six

1. Quran; Surah Al-'Araaf (#7 The Heights):172 and Footnote #1146 in Yusuf Ali's Translation of the Meaning

2. Ibid.; Surah Ali 'Imran (#3 The Family of Imran):103

3. Refer to Bell's Theorem and Laws of Quantum Physics; An invisible stream of energy remains between two objects, once they are connected.

4. Sayyid Sabiq; Fiqh Us-Sunnah; Book of Salaat; p. 201

5. Quran; Surah Al-Baqarah (#2 The Cow):260

6. E.W.. Jensen; Families: A Routine Inventory; Social Science and Medicine; Vol. 7:1993; pp. 210-211

7. Literally "night of power"; A night in the last ten nights of the month of Ramadan. In Quran it is described as "better than one thousand months". See Surah 97.

8. Yusuf Ali; The Holy Quran - Translation of Its Meaning and

Commentary; Footnote #44278 to Chapter 39:23; p. 1402

9. Quran; Surah Al-Baqarah (#2 The Cow):186

10. Sunan of Abu Dawood; Hadith No. 1102 and Ibn Katheer; Tafseer of Quran; Note to Surah 8:65 -66

11. Sahih Muslim; Collection of Hadith; ; or Riyadh As-Saliheen; p. 449: #847

12. Quran; Surah Al-Fussilat (#41 The Detailed Explanation): 33-34

13. Muhammad bin Muhammad Al-Ghazali; Ihyaa Uloom Ud-Deen; Vol. 3

14. Sahih Bukharee; Collection of Hadith; Vol. 8:No. 246; p.160

15. Ibid.; Vol.8:No. 250; p. 165

16. Quran; Surah An-Nisaa (#4 The Women):Ayah 86

17. Ibid.; Surah Ali 'Imraan (#3 The Family of 'Imraan):110

18. Ibid.; Surah Ali 'Imraan:139

19. Quran; Surah Al-Ma'idah (#5 The Tablespread):55

20. Ibid.; Surah Rum (#30 Rome):21

21. Ibid.; Surah Al-Ma'idah (#5 The Tablespread):6

22. Ibid.; Surah An-Nisaa (#4 The Women):79

23. Istikharah is a supplication for seeking guidance in forming a decision or choosing a course of action. It is found in "Supplications From Quran and Sunnah" compiled by Saeed Ibn Ali and also in Du'ah From Quran and Sunnah by Jamal Badawi.

24. Carolyn Myss; Anatomy of The Spirit; Harmony Books; 1996; p.130

25. Paul Pearsall; The Heart's Code; Broadway Books; 1998; p. 158

26. Quran; Surah Al-Anbiyaa (#21 The Prophets):18

27. Paul Pearsall; The Heart's Code; Broadway Books; 1998; p. 191

End Notes

Chapter Seven

1. An-Nawawi's Forty Hadith: An Anthology; No. 6

2. Quran; Surah Al-Inshiqaq (#84 The Splitting Asunder): 16 - 19

3. Jafar Idris; Process of Islamization; Maryland International Graphics; 1977; p. 4

4. Surah Al-Qiyammah (#75 The Resurrection):Ayah 2

5. Abdul Fattah R. Hamid; Self Knowledge and Spiritual Yearning; ATP

6. Quran; Surah Al-Faatir (#35 The Originator of Creation):Ayah 18

7. Ibid.; Surah Yusuf (#12 Joseph):Ayah 53

8. An Nawawi's Forty Hadith: An Anthology; No. 1

9. The Purification of the Soul; Collected and Arranged by Ahmed Farid; Al-Firdaus Ltd.; London; 1993

10. Quran; Surah Al-Saffat (#37 Those Arranged In Ranks):Ayat 83-86

11. Paul Pearsall; The Heart's Code; Broadway Books; 1998

12. Don Campbell; The Mozart Effect; Avon Books; 1997; p. 53

13. Quran; Surah Al-Raad (#13 The Thunder):Ayah 27-28

14. Old Testament; Book of Psalms; Psalm 37:4

15. Quran; Surah Al-Shu'araa (#26 The Poets):Ayat 83-89

Our hearts are the centers of feeling and emotion.
Clearly what our hearts' experience
Are the reasons for world propulsion.
The heart never forgets that which is
Done with mean spirit or a beautiful act.
It calculates and It's measurements are exact.
As the heart pulsates our bodies are committed to action.
Those hearts which follow that
Which gives Peace and Serenity
Will surely be those of satisfaction.

Ayanna Nalini

QUICK ORDER FORM
PO Box 30762 ~ Columbia, MO 65205-3762
(573) 214-2181
www.omspublishing.com

Olive
media
Services

Postal Order: Send this form to address above.

Call for volume discounts!
Credit Card orders may be placed on Amazon.com.

Please send the following books:

Book Title	Quantity	Total
_____	_____	_____
_____	_____	_____

Please Send Information on:
Other books   Lectures/Seminars/Radio Shows

Name: _____

Address: _____

City _____ State: _____ Zip: _____

Telephone: _____

E mail Address: _____

Sales Tax: Please add 5.225% for shipment to Missouri addresses.

Shipping by USPS Priority Mail:
Add $3.50 for the first book and $1.00 for each additional product.

157

Olive Media Services

Publishing for a better humanity

"Understand, as stated before, we are not defining 'mind' as it is commonly understood, that is, as a capacity of the brain, but from the Quranic and newly proposed sceientific perspective as being directed and dominated by the heart."

ABOUT THE AUTHOR

Jeanette L'amour Hablullah, N.D. is a Muslim American, who chose Islam as a way of life after many years as a Catholic. She began formal study of Wholistic Therapies in Indianapolis, IN in 1992 under the tutelage of Dr. Cristina Brown at The Academy of Reflexology and Holistic Therapy International. It was during this time that her own natural gift of healing insight and ability to channel energy began to emerge. In 1995, after attaining a Doctor of Naturopathy degree from Clayton College of Natural Healing, she opened the independent office of The Pearl Within.

Dr. Hablullah continues to practice and give lectures, workshops, and seminars on Wholistic Healing and Islamic topics.

ABOUT THE ARTIST

Alaa El-Buri is the second of five daughters. She is currently studying at the University of Missouri. She is pursuing a major in International Affairs and plans to continue her education in law school. Alaa plans to devote her time and efforts for the benefit of the Muslim Ummah (Community) in the United States and abroad.